THE Ultimate KIDS' BAKING BOOK

60 EASY & FUN DESSERT RECIPES
for Every Holiday, Birthday, Milestone and More

THE
Ultimate
KIDS'
BAKING
BOOK

Tiffany Dahle

author of
The Ultimate Kids' Cookbook

PAGE STREET
PUBLISHING CO.

PAGE STREET
PUBLISHING CO.

Copyright © 2019 Tiffany Dahle

First published in 2019 by
Page Street Publishing Co.
27 Congress Street, Suite 105
Salem, MA 01970
www.pagestreetpublishing.com

Distributed by Macmillan, sales in Canada by The Canadian Manda Group.

24   23   22   21   20   3   4   5   6   7

ISBN-13: 978-1-62414-878-1
ISBN-10: 1-62414-878-6

Library of Congress Control Number: 2019940339

Cover and book design by Meg Baskis for Page Street Publishing Co.
Photography by Tiffany Dahle
Auhor photo by Carissa Rogers Photography

Printed and bound in the United States

FOR ALL THE

Magic Makers

"Those that don't believe in magic will never find it."

–ROALD DAHL

CONTENTS

HEY KIDS,
THIS NOTE'S FOR YOU!

Lean in close for a second; I have a secret to tell you . . .

You have the power to make magic.

Don't believe me?

Have you ever seen someone's face light up when they bite into the most delicious cookie they've ever tasted?

Or have you heard the sound of contented sighs as they bite into a rich and delicious birthday cake covered with their favorite color icing?

Maybe you've smelled melting chocolate or hot cinnamon when you walked in the door after school and felt your own spirits lift.

That's magic. And it's right there in front of us! YOU have the power to make that happen for those you love.

The cookies my daughters bake for me taste better than any other cookies! I know it is because food magically tastes better when it is made by someone who loves you.

Even if you've never baked before, the treats I'm going to teach you to make for your family and friends will be the best they've ever tasted because they come with your love baked inside.

I specially chose our family's very favorite desserts for holidays all year round that would give you the greatest chance for kitchen success. But I hope you know that when you learn to bake, you are not trying to compete with the pictures. They are just there to inspire you and give you some ideas for how the final treat can look. There is plenty of room for you to make the dessert your own!

Change the colors, change the cookie cutout shape, add your own signature sprinkle blend. Have fun playing with these treats and add your own special brand of magic to them.

Now, strap on your apron. Grab your whisk. And be sure to sprinkle a little "pixie dust" over everything you make.

Cheers!

Miss Tiffany

HEY PARENTS,
THIS NOTE'S FOR YOU!

The heavy metallic thud of a stand mixer landing into place on the kitchen counter and the light, tinny rattle of cookie canisters being retrieved from the farthest corner of the cabinet immediately bring me back to the magic of my childhood Christmases.

My mom made each holiday special, but Christmas was her grand finale. I remember a sea of treats cooling on the counter waiting to fill those cookie tins.

She always told my sister and me that life is better when you have something to look forward to. For us, her favorite sweet holidays were a constant rotation of simple celebrations that sparked great joy all year long. When one holiday finished, another was coming up right behind it. She always gave us something to look forward to.

Today, some of my very favorite memories involve time spent in the kitchen baking with my daughters for those same sweet and simple holidays. When we are working on a recipe, it isn't "my treat" or "their treat"; it is our group project that everyone is eager to slice into and taste as a family.

Although the recipes in this book are written to be easy enough for your kids to follow along with on their own, you still have a coveted place at their side! Today's modern families struggle with overburdened, busy schedules. When you carve out some time to slow down and share a moment in the kitchen, you'll have not only an opportunity to teach valuable life skills, but enjoy some priceless technology-free bonding time with your kids.

You'll quickly discover that your children have the desire to be real holiday helpers. You will see their faces glow with pride bringing their delicious contribution to your next celebratory feast. I know the holiday magic-making may have fallen mostly on your shoulders while they were tiny, but now's the time to bring your kids into the fold. Teach them your festive tips and tricks, share your favorite holiday recipes and discover some new family favorites after testing a treat or two from this book! Connecting with your kids is the true key to making the holidays memorable for each of you.

But don't wait for the next big calendar holiday to get started! I hope you'll be encouraged by these recipes to find dozens of everyday opportunities to celebrate with your family. My treats are designed to please every single one of you from the youngest kid right on up to Grandma and Grandpa. They will work seamlessly into your family's favorite festive traditions and hopefully inspire you to start cherished new ones.

Becoming BAKERS

Are you ready to become a baker? If you've dreamed about making custom cupcakes for parties or wowing your friends with awesome cookies, you're definitely in the right spot.

Before you jump in with both oven mitts, there are a few things you should know.

STEP 1: BE PREPARED

Read the WHOLE recipe through before you choose something to bake.

Ask yourself these questions as you read through the instructions:

Do I have all the ingredients?

Does our kitchen have all the equipment I need?

Do any of the ingredients, such as butter or cream cheese, need time to soften?

Does the dough require chilling? For how long?

Does the recipe require sitting in the fridge to set? For how long?

Recipes for baking are not like recipes for cooking. With baking, you need to follow the instructions carefully from beginning to end. You will need to use the exact ingredients in the exact quantities, or the baked treat may not turn out correctly. There is a lot more flexibility with cooking to swap ingredients, but if you miss something in a baked good, you may discover your cake doesn't rise or your cookies fall apart. However, there are some cases where you can substitute something specific for an ingredient you are missing. Be sure to check out page 183 where we list some really helpful swaps that will save you from asking for a trip to the grocery store!

When you read through your recipe, be sure to look at the timing for each step. Nothing is worse than discovering your recipe needs to chill for four hours but your party starts in one hour! Be sure to think through the timing of your baking window and how long you have until you plan to eat your treat.

Some treats require assembly-line production. When you read through the instructions, check out the tools and dishes you will need before you begin and set them out where you can grab them as needed.

To help guide you through each recipe, you'll find special icons throughout the recipes:

 BE CAREFUL! These recipes will have a step or two with extra hot ingredients. Watch your fingers.

 CHILL IT! These recipes will require time in the fridge to set or cool.

 MAKE IT AHEAD! These recipes can be made a day or two in advance which will help save time. Or the treat can be stored in the freezer for later. For example, you can bake the whole batch of cookies now and freeze the extras to enjoy later.

 TAKE IT ALONG! These recipes are great for taking on the go. If the party is somewhere other than your house, pick one of these!

STEP 2
HOW MUCH DO YOU NEED?

How many people do you plan to feed with your treat? Every recipe will tell you how many servings you will end up making.

IF YOU NEED MORE: When you want to double a recipe (i.e., to make two times the amount), it is usually a better idea to make the recipe two separate times rather than pour twice the ingredients into the mixing bowls at once. Smaller batches are easier to work with than big ones. You don't want your ingredients spilling over the edges of the mixing bowl!

IF YOU NEED LESS: Some recipes can easily be cut in half to make a smaller amount, but it can affect the baking time for cakes and bars. It is usually a better idea to make the whole recipe now and store some of your treats in the freezer for another time. This works especially well with cookies or unfrosted cupcakes.

STEP 3
SAFETY FIRST!

The most important thing of all is to be mindful of your safety. Baking is generally safer than cooking since there is less chopping and use of the stovetop. However, there are several things you should be especially careful of with baking.

We recommend these recipes for kids aged ten and up, but if you're younger than that, just check to see whether an adult can help you with anything especially hot.

OVEN SAFETY: Be careful every time you open the oven. Stand back and let the first puff of heat escape before you put your face near the open door. Always wear oven mitts when putting anything into or taking something out of the oven. The door and the racks get very hot—you don't want to accidentally bump either one with your bare hands.

STOVETOP SAFETY: Whenever you boil or melt something on the stovetop, be sure to use long-handled spoons and spatulas to keep your hands away from the hot liquids. Turn the handles of the pots away from the heat and in a position where you won't accidentally bump them. This is especially important if you have younger siblings or lively pets in the kitchen.

MICROWAVE SAFETY: Many recipes use a microwave oven for melting ingredients. Always use oven mitts when taking something out of a microwave. Glass and ceramic dishes can get very hot. You may find that the ingredients inside the dish have melted unevenly with superhot pockets mixed in. Stir the melting ingredients slowly and carefully so the hot portions don't splash onto your hands.

Also, never put anything metal inside a microwave. It will cause fiery sparks. Double-check that your container is microwave safe. Ask an adult if you are unsure.

CUTTING SAFELY: Most recipes in this book will not require anything sharper than a butter knife from your utensil drawer. If you find you are struggling to cut something with that simple knife, it is time to stop and ask for help from an adult.

STEP 4
DON'T FORGET TO CLEAN UP!

Your parents will support your desire to bake if they know the kitchen won't be destroyed in the process. Remember where all the ingredients came from in your kitchen so you can put them back in the right spot. Throw away any used wrappers or packaging. Wash your utensils and dishes and put them away. And don't forget to wipe the counters!

WHEN TO ASK FOR HELP

In the kitchen, it is always better to ask for help from an adult than to struggle trying to do it yourself. If you feel uncomfortable about any step, ask an adult to show you how to do it properly. Most times, you'll only need to be shown once and then will be able to do it yourself the next time. If you've never used a certain appliance or tool before, such as a microwave or an electric mixer, have an adult give you a tour of the buttons and how it works. You'll be an expert in no time.

STOCKING A KID-FRIENDLY KITCHEN

The tools we use in our kitchen most often, and which are featured in many of the recipes, include:

- **ELECTRIC MIXER:** Either a hand mixer or stand mixer with a paddle attachment will work for most recipes.

- **WHISK:** This is important for stirring air into your recipes. We like both the metal and silicone varieties.

- **GLASS MEASURING CUPS:** We use a 2-cup (473-ml) measuring cup for melting ingredients in a microwave as well as measuring liquids. It works great for cracking eggs separately, too.

- **NESTED MIXING BOWLS:** Small, medium and large come in handy for prepping ingredients. We love a large (5-quart [4.7-L]-capacity bowl for mixing. A 3-quart (2.8-L) and a 1½-quart (1.4-L) bowl are good sizes for the medium and small prep bowls, but you can use whatever you have in your kitchen.

- **SPATULAS:** We like both a flat spatula for scooping cookies off a cookie pan as well as a spoon-shaped spatula for stirring batter and scraping down bowls.

- **BUTTER KNIFE:** A regular butter knife from your utensil drawer will cut most things.

- **EGG SEPARATOR:** This is a superhandy gadget, but we have a trick for separating eggs without it on page 30.

- **PARCHMENT PAPER:** It's always great to line a cookie pan with parchment paper to prevent sticking. It works well to line counters under wire racks for decorating cookies, too.

BAKING PAN GUIDE

Be sure you're using the correct baking pan for the job! How do you know? These pans are featured throughout the book:

- **COOKIE PAN, AKA COOKIE SHEET:** A large flat pan with or without a rimmed border. They come in varying sizes, but we tested our recipes on sheets 12 x 17 inches (30.5 x 43 cm).

- **JELLY-ROLL PAN:** Looks just like a cookie pan but has a 1-inch (2.5-cm) rim all around the border. The most useful and common size is 12 x 17 inches (30.5 x 43 cm).

- **9-INCH (23-CM) SQUARE BAKING PAN:** A baking dish made of metal, ceramic or glass.

- **9 X 13-INCH (23 X 33-CM) RECTANGULAR BAKING PAN:** A baking dish made of metal, ceramic or glass.

- **PIE PAN:** A round baking dish with a 2- to 3-inch (5- to 7.5-cm) slanted rim, made of metal, ceramic or glass. We use a 9-inch (23-cm)-diameter pie pan for our recipes; you might have to adjust the baking time to be a little shorter if your pan is bigger.

- **BUNDTLETTE PAN:** A pan with 6 round wells that form tiny cakes that look like tall, decorative donuts.

- **DONUT PAN:** A metal pan with 6 round, shallow wells shaped to form donuts.

- **MUFFIN TIN:** A metal pan with 12 wells used to make cupcakes or muffins.

HOLIDAY INDEX: "THERE'S ALWAYS SOMETHING TO CELEBRATE!"

Every family has unique days they want to enjoy together. Here's a list of some popular holidays and the recipes we love to go with them.

NATIONAL POPCORN DAY (JANUARY 19)

- Birthday Cake Popcorn (page 70)
- Reindeer Munch (page 167) with winter-colored sprinkles

VALENTINE'S DAY (FEBRUARY 14)

- Chocolate-Covered Strawberry Brownies (page 76)
- Simply Sweet Sugar Cookies (page 66), heart shaped
- Sprinkle-Dipped Crispy Treats (page 73), with pink and red sprinkles
- Classic Buttery Yellow Cupcakes (page 50), with pink-tinted Sweet Buttercream Frosting (page 38)

100TH DAY OF SCHOOL

- Simply Sweet Sugar Cookies (page 66), cut into 1s and 0s
- Fluffernutter Muddy Buddies (page 113), counted out into bags of 100 pieces

ST. PATRICK'S DAY (MARCH 17)

- Luck o' the Irish Chocolate Cupcakes (page 82)
- Simply Sweet Sugar Cookies (page 66), clover shaped with green icing
- Spring Green Pistachio Torte (page 90)
- Grasshopper Torte (page 121)

MARDI GRAS

- Classic Buttery Yellow Cupcakes (page 50), with purple- and green-tinted Sweet Buttercream Frosting (page 38) and golden sprinkles
- Birthday Sprinkle Donuts (page 69)
- Red, White and Blueberry Poke Cake (page 122), using purple and green gelatin and omitting the fruit

APRIL FOOL'S DAY (APRIL 1)

- Hot Fudge Sundae Cupcakes (page 105)
- All-American Potato Chip Cookies (page 110)

EARTH DAY (APRIL 22)

- Earth Day Dirt Cups (page 85)
- Custom Color Cookie Bars (page 65), with blue and green M&M's
- Luck o' the Irish Chocolate Cupcakes (page 82), with green and blue frosting

EASTER

- Carrot Cake Donuts (page 93)
- Dainty Daisy Cupcakes (page 89)
- Hummingbird Cupcakes (page 97)
- Bird's Nest Haystack Cookies (page 86)

- Tropical Lime Cookies (page 94)
- Drop Biscuits with Cinnamon-Honey Butter (page 98) and Sweet and Smooth Strawberry Jam Sauce (page 44)
- Sunshine Bars (page 114)

STAR WARS DAY (MAY 4)

- Simply Sweet Sugar Cookies (page 66), star shaped
- New Year's Eve Brownie Ball Drop Pops (page 175), with galaxy sprinkles

MOTHER'S DAY

- Hummingbird Cupcakes (page 97)
- Drop Biscuits with Cinnamon-Honey Butter (page 98) and Sweet and Smooth Strawberry Jam Sauce (page 44)
- Sunshine Bars (page 114)
- The Best Birthday Cake for the One Who Bakes for You (page 57)
- Spring Green Pistachio Torte (page 90)
- Chocolate-Covered Strawberry Brownies (page 76)

FATHER'S DAY

- Father's Day Pretzel Bark (page 109)
- All-American Potato Chip Cookies (page 110)
- Pancake Donuts with Maple Glaze (page 117)
- Chocolate Scotcheroos (page 176)

LAST DAY OF SCHOOL/FIRST DAY OF SUMMER

- Strawberry Icebox Dessert (page 102)
- Grasshopper Torte (page 121)
- Simply Sweet Sugar Cookies (page 66), shining sun and beach ball shaped
- Tropical Lime Cookies (page 94)

PATRIOTIC PARTIES (MEMORIAL DAY OR 4TH OF JULY)

- Mini Pi Day Pies (page 79)
- Red, White and Blueberry Poke Cake (page 122)
- Simply Sweet Sugar Cookies (page 66), with Sweet Buttercream Frosting (page 38) and fresh berries
- New Year's Eve Brownie Ball Drop Pops (page 175), with red, white and blue jimmies

LONGEST DAY OF THE YEAR (JUNE 21)

- Sunshine Bars (page 114)
- Red, White and Blueberry Poke Cake (page 122), with orange and lemon gelatin, blueberries omitted, topped with mandarin oranges
- Classic Buttery Yellow Cupcakes (page 50), with orange-tinted Sweet Buttercream Frosting (page 38)

SUMMER READING PICNICS

- Pancake Donuts with Maple Glaze (page 117)
- Drop Biscuits with Cinnamon-Honey Butter (page 98)

NATIONAL ICE CREAM DAY (3RD SUNDAY IN JULY)

- Grasshopper Torte (page 121)
- Hot Fudge Sundae Cupcakes (page 105)

FAMILY ROAD TRIPS

- Malted Chocolate Chip Cookies (page 106)
- Fluffernutter Muddy Buddies (page 113)
- S'mores Bars (page 118)
- Scrumptious Snickerdoodles (page 144)

FRIENDSHIP DAY (AUGUST 4)

- Marvelous Movie Candy Cookies (page 143)
- Giant Birthday Cookie Cake (page 54)
- Birthday Cake Popcorn (page 70)

FIRST DAY OF SCHOOL

- Smart Cookies (page 139)
- Fluffernutter Muddy Buddies (page 113)
- Apple Cider Donuts (page 129)
- Chocolate Scotcheroos (page 176)

THE BIG GAME

- Fluffernutter Muddy Buddies (page 113)
- All-American Potato Chip Cookies (page 110)
- Father's Day Pretzel Bark (page 109)
- Strawberry Pretzel Cheesecake Bars (page 140)

GRANDPARENTS DAY (SEPTEMBER 8)

- Spring Green Pistachio Torte (page 90)
- Hummingbird Cupcakes (page 97)
- Ginormous Elegant Elephant Ears (page 132)
- Epic Chocolate Layer Cake (page 58)

FAMILY MOVIE NIGHT

- Marvelous Movie Candy Cookies (page 143)
- Birthday Cake Popcorn (page 70)
- Fluffernutter Muddy Buddies (page 113)
- Reindeer Munch (page 167)

ROSH HASHANAH

- Mini Pi Day Pies (page 79), apple, with honey
- Apple Cider Donuts (page 129), with honey

HALLOWEEN (OCTOBER 31)

- Candy Corn Fudge (page 152)
- Witch's Cauldron Brownie Bites (page 148)
- Chocolate Eyeball Truffles (page 151)
- Custom Color Cookie Bars (page 65), orange and black

THANKSGIVING (4TH THURSDAY IN NOVEMBER)

- Frosted Cranberry Bliss Bundtlettes (page 126)
- Thankful-for-You Cake Pop Bouquet (page 136)
- Ginormous Elegant Elephant Ears (page 132)
- Gingerbread Cookie Cutouts (page 159), with Cream Cheese Frosting (page 42)
- Drop Biscuits with Cinnamon-Honey Butter (page 98)

NATIONAL COOKIE DAY (DECEMBER 4)

- Crinkle Cookies (page 163)
- Spritz Cookies (page 164)
- Gingerbread Cookie Cutouts (page 159)
- Simply Sweet Sugar Cookies (page 66)
- Snowball Cookies (page 179)
- Scrumptious Snickerdoodles (page 144)
- Smart Cookies (page 139)
- Malted Chocolate Chip Cookies (page 106)
- All-American Potato Chip Cookies (page 110)
- Tropical Lime Cookies (page 94)

HANUKKAH

- Confetti Cupcake Cuties (page 53), with blue and silver sprinkles
- Simply Sweet Sugar Cookies (page 66), Star of David shaped
- Sprinkle-Dipped Crispy Treats (page 73), with blue sprinkles

CHRISTMAS EVE (DECEMBER 24)

- Sticky Pudding Trifle Parfaits (page 168)
- Reindeer Munch (page 167)
- Gingerbread Cookie Cutouts (page 159)
- Spritz Cookies (page 164)
- Crinkle Cookies (page 163)
- Sparkle Cupcakes (page 172)

CHRISTMAS DAY (DECEMBER 25)

- Red Velvet Donuts with Cream Cheese Glaze (page 156)
- Mini Monkey Bread Muffins (page 171)
- Spring Green Pistachio Torte (page 90)
- Chocolate-Covered Strawberry Brownies (page 76)
- Strawberry Pretzel Cheesecake Bars (page 140)
- Frosted Cranberry Bliss Bundtlettes (page 126)

NEW YEAR'S EVE (DECEMBER 31)

- New Year's Eve Brownie Ball Drop Pops (page 175)
- Sparkle Cupcakes (page 172)
- Simply Sweet Sugar Cookies (page 66), star shaped
- Sprinkle-Dipped Crispy Treats (page 73)

NEW YEAR'S DAY (JANUARY 1)

- Mini Monkey Bread Muffins (page 171)
- Apple Cider Donuts (page 129)
- Snowball Cookies (page 179)

SNOW DAY

- Chocolate Scotcheroos (page 176)
- Snowball Cookies (page 179)
- Smart Cookies (page 139)
- Scrumptious Snickerdoodles (page 144)
- Crinkle Cookies (page 163)
- Marvelous Movie Candy Cookies (page 143)

GOTCHA DAY

- Epic Chocolate Layer Cake (page 58)
- The Best Birthday Cake for the One Who Bakes for You (page 57)
- Confetti Cupcake Cuties (page 53)
- Giant Birthday Cookie Cake (page 54)

HALF BIRTHDAYS

- Birthday Cake Popcorn (page 70)
- Birthday Sprinkle Donuts (page 69)
- Simply Sweet Sugar Cookies (page 66), balloon shaped

BAKING
School

There are a few really important skills you need to bake up any delicious treat. Once you learn them, you'll discover you use them over and over again in the recipes throughout this book.

In this chapter, you'll learn the skills all the best bakers need to know: how to beat butter and sugar together, how to separate eggs, how to space cookies on a pan and even awesome decorating tips for beginners.

As you work through the skills, keep imagining how beautiful your final dessert is going to look. The best treats start with careful preparation, and with our sneaky little tips and tricks, you'll be whipping up amazing cakes in no time.

JIMMIES

CONFETTI SPRINKLES OR QUINS

NONPAREILS

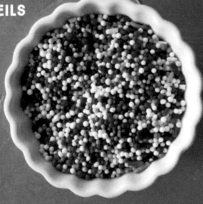

CRYSTAL SUGAR

THE MAGIC MAKERS' GUIDE TO PARTY SPRINKLES

Shimmering and shiny or colorful and crunchy, choosing the just-right sprinkle before you even get started will help you plan a perfectly sweet masterpiece with the exact finishing touch it needs. Sprinkles are not an afterthought; they are the inspiration for our entire design! But with endless options available, how do you know which one to choose?

These are the sprinkles we highly recommend:

JIMMIES: The most-used classic party sprinkle looks like a joyful fireworks display. They come in a rainbow of colors; you can likely find just what you need at the grocery store. You can bake jimmies inside a cake or use them on top of frosting.

CONFETTI SPRINKLES OR QUINS: These slightly crunchy, flat sprinkles are what you find in many funfetti cupcakes. They can be round or come in fun shapes such as stars and hearts. They are perfect for using inside or on top of your treat. The baking section at your craft store will likely have them or you can order them online.

NONPAREILS: These crunchy and tiny round balls come in a wide variety of colors and metallic finishes. They are best used on top of your treat and not inside; the colors tend to run when baked or swirled into frosting. Several options are usually available at the grocery store.

CRYSTAL SUGAR: These clear, icy-looking, cubelike sprinkles make any treat glitter. They are used as a finishing touch, not as an ingredient inside your treat. You can find several color options at the grocery store or baking department in a craft store.

HOW TO DECORATE WITH SPRINKLES

Although they are the cutest accessory, you may not always want to cover the entire top of your treat with sprinkles. Sometimes they are better just as an accent. Here are our favorite ways to use sprinkles:

- Just around the border of a cake or cupcake.

- Over half of a cookie: Use a piece of parchment paper to cover one-half of the cookie for a decorative effect.

- Place a tiny cookie cutter shape on top of your treat, fill it with a thin layer of sprinkles and carefully lift the cutter straight up to reveal your fun design.

- Dip or roll a cake pop in a small cup of sprinkles.

- Make a custom blend: Mix and match two or more types of sprinkles in a variety of colors to match your theme.

- Press a few extra sprinkles into the top of cookies or cookie bars before baking; they'll show better than the ones that were stirred into the raw batter.

BUTTER MAKES IT BETTER!

One of the most important ingredients in baking is butter. You'll find it in just about every cookie and it is the base for most frostings. Butter gives your desserts flavor, moisture and shape.

However, you shouldn't just take a stick of butter out of the fridge and pop it into your mixing bowl. Before you get baking, here's everything you need to know about using butter.

HOW TO MEASURE BUTTER

You'll find that a pound (450 g) of butter is usually sold as four long sticks individually wrapped in paper. Each stick is 8 tablespoons or ½ cup (112 g). The lines on the side of the wrapper will mark each tablespoon (14 g).

You can use a butter knife to cut the portion of butter you need for your recipe by counting the number of tablespoons necessary on the paper wrapping. You can cut right through the paper and return the still-wrapped portion you don't need back to the fridge for another time.

HOW TO SOFTEN BUTTER

Most recipes require the butter to be softened. This means leaving the butter on a plate on your kitchen counter until it warms up to the same temperature as your room. You can tell the butter is ready if you press a finger *gently* into the top of the butter and your finger leaves an indentation. This can take an hour or more, so be sure to read your recipe and plan ahead.

Some microwaves have a butter-softening feature that can save you time. Ask your parents to help you with the settings, if your microwave can do this.

HOW TO MELT BUTTER

Some recipes require melted butter. We love to use regular Pyrex glass measuring cups with a spout, for melting our butter in the microwave. Just place the unwrapped butter you need in the measuring cup, and cover it lightly with a small square of paper towel or waxed paper to prevent splatters. Place the cup in the microwave and heat for 20-second sessions until the butter is melted. Be sure to use oven mitts when removing the hot cup!

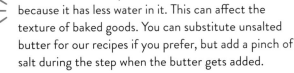

NOTE: Our recipes were tested with regular salted butter, since that is likely what you already have on hand. Some bakers prefer to use unsalted butter because it has less water in it. This can affect the texture of baked goods. You can substitute unsalted butter for our recipes if you prefer, but add a pinch of salt during the step when the butter gets added.

1 TBSP | 2 TBSP | 3 TBSP | 4 TBSP | 5 TBSP | 6 TBSP | 7 TBSP | 8 TBSP

1/4 CUP | 1/3 CUP | 8 TBSP = 1 STICK = 1/2 CUP

NET WT. 4 OZ. (113g)

THIS UNIT NOT LABELED FOR INDIVIDUAL SALE

787578
© 2017 LAND O'LAKES, INC.
A PRODUCT OF LAND O'LAKES, INC., ARDEN HILLS, MN 55126

LET'S MIX IT UP!

Many recipes require using a mixer to combine ingredients. There are two mixers you might find in your kitchen:

A LARGE STAND MIXER: This kitchen appliance has an arm with a beating blade that lifts and lowers and a large mixing bowl that attaches to the base.

A SMALL HAND MIXER: This smaller appliance is handheld with two beaters that attach to the base. If you are using a hand mixer, you will need to find a large mixing bowl for beating your ingredients together. A large bowl made of metal, glass or ceramic is the best choice for working with a hand mixer.

HOW TO CREAM BUTTER AND SUGAR

Beating butter and sugar together, also called creaming, is a very common first step for many baked goods. Place your softened butter (see page 24) in the mixing bowl and pour in the sugar you need. Use your mixer to beat them together until they are light and fluffy, about 2 to 3 minutes.

Creaming butter makes it smooth and blends the sugar all throughout the batter. It adds air to the mixture that will help keep your treats light, too.

HOW TO SCRAPE THE MIXING BOWL

Both kinds of mixers will beat the ingredients up the sides of the mixing bowl. To ensure that everything is well mixed, it is important to use a spatula to scrape down the sides of your bowl a few times through the mixing stages.

1. Turn your mixer off.

2. Lift the arm of the stand mixer or remove the hand mixer blades from the bowl.

3. Carefully use the back of a spatula or spoonula to scrape and push all the ingredients clinging to the wall of the bowl down toward the center.

4. Scrape as much as you can get off the beating blades over the mixing bowl.

5. Lower the stand mixer arm or return the hand mixer to the bowl and continue to beat the ingredients until well blended.

SLOW DOWN, SPEEDY!

It is always smart to start with a low speed and slowly increase the speed as the mixer is working. If you go from stopped to full speed, all your ingredients will fly out of the bowl! Start on speed setting 1 or 2 and slowly work your way up from there as needed.

HOMEMADE WHIPPED CREAM

YIELD: 2 CUPS (473 ML) WHIPPED CREAM

The perfect finishing touch for many desserts is a little dollop of whipped cream. It adds a creamy burst of sweetness that highlights the other flavors of your treat. Making your own whipped cream is so very easy! The best part is that not only is homemade whipped cream way more delicious than the store-bought variety, but you can customize the perfect accent for your masterpiece by using extracts for just the right flavor. How about a vanilla whipped cream to go with the pumpkin pie on page 135? Or maybe you need a peppermint whipped cream to top your holiday trifles on page 168.

2 tbsp (26 g) sugar

1 cup (237 ml) heavy whipping cream

OPTIONAL FLAVOR ADDITIONS (CHOOSE JUST ONE)

1 tsp vanilla extract

½ tsp peppermint extract

½ tsp almond extract

Swap the sugar for 2 tbsp (30 ml) maple syrup and ¼ tsp vanilla extract

2 tbsp (30 ml) chocolate or strawberry-flavored syrups

A metal bowl is the best option for making homemade whipped cream. You can whip it by hand with a metal whisk, but it will be a lot easier with your mixer with the whisk attachment. Place the bowl and whisk you plan to use inside the freezer for 10 minutes. Keep the cream inside the fridge up until the moment you plan to use it.

In the chilled bowl, combine the sugar, cream and any flavor additions you want to use. Whisk vigorously by hand or on high with your mixer until the cream thickens and starts to form stiff peaks. A stiff peak is when you gently poke the whipped cream with your whisk, lift your whisk away and a peak forms. If it holds its pointy shape, the whipped cream is ready. If the point falls back down into the cream, whisk it a little more. Be careful to stop whisking when you see the peaks. If you whisk too much, it will become chunky.

NOTE: Be sure to make the whipped cream on the same day you plan to use it. You can store it in the fridge in an air-tight container for up to 10 hours, but then it will deflate.

AN EGGSCELLENT PLACE TO START

Eggs are like the glue that holds baked treats together. Usually we use the whole egg, but some recipes call for just the white or just the yolk. Always double check your recipe before you begin.

When baking with eggs, here are a few handy tips you'll need:

HOW TO REMOVE EGGSHELL FROM A CRACKED EGG

We always recommend cracking your egg into a separate small bowl and not directly into the main mixing bowl. This lets you check for shells and, if necessary, remove them before they hide inside your treat. No one wants to bite a cupcake and get an eggshell! If a small piece gets into your cracked egg, simply use one of the cracked eggshell halves like a spoon to scoop up the broken bit. You'll find it works almost like a magnet to catch the broken piece!

HOW TO SEPARATE THE EGG YOLK FROM THE EGG WHITE

If your recipe calls for just the yolk or just the egg white, you will need to separate them. You can find handy egg-separating tools for $5, but if you don't have that gadget, you can also use a pair of cereal spoons.

1. Crack the egg into a small measuring cup with a spout. Be careful you don't break the yolk.

2. Place a small bowl on your counter, hold one of the spoons level over the bowl and then carefully pour the egg into the spoon.

3. Catch the yolk with the spoon and let the egg whites run into the bowl.

4. Then, very gently transfer the egg yolk to the second spoon, letting the whites continue to run into the bowl.

5. Use the portion of the egg you need and discard the rest.

HOW TO MIX HOT INGREDIENTS WITH RAW EGGS

If your recipe calls for a hot ingredient (such as melted butter or chocolate, or heated milk) and eggs, be careful NOT to pour all of the hot liquid directly onto the raw egg or it will begin to cook. It is better to briefly combine the batter with the egg alone and then slowly drizzle in the hot liquid while beating or stirring. This lets the hot ingredient cool a bit and won't overwhelm your raw egg.

BE GENTLE, DON'T OVERBEAT YOUR EGGS

Many recipes warn to beat your eggs into the batter until "just combined." If you overbeat the eggs, the whites can become stiff and dry and affect your final recipe texture. Just mix the batter until it is evenly wet with no dry pockets and then stop!

FOLDING ISN'T JUST FOR PAPER

Some special treats have delicate ingredients, such as sprinkles or whipped egg whites, which need to be mixed with heavier, thicker ingredients, such as rich cookie dough or cake batter. If you just toss everything into the bowl at once, those fragile ingredients can end up crushed and broken or you might find you've popped all the air bubbles that were supposed to make your cake light and fluffy.

To incorporate delicate ingredients into a batter, we use a stirring trick called folding.

Folding is always done by hand with a spoon or spatula. If you used a stand mixer to mix your ingredients before this step, you'll want to raise the arm and scrape any batter or dough from the blade first. Don't use the mixer to fold; it will be too rough on the delicate ingredients. It's easiest to simply remove the mixing bowl from the stand once the thick batter is mixed and then do the folding step with the bowl set directly on your counter.

Add the ingredient you want to fold into your thick batter in the mixing bowl. Gently and slowly stir the batter from the bottom of the bowl up. Rotate your spoon around the edge of the bowl and then down to the bottom again. As you stir and lift your spoon, fold the batter over onto itself. Continue to gently rotate the spoon down and around the batter and lift it over itself again until your delicate ingredient has been folded in evenly throughout the batter.

Ingredients that are often folded into batter:

- Candies (such as M&M's)
- Chocolate chips
- Sprinkles
- Blueberries or other delicate fruits
- Nuts
- Whipped cream or whipped topping
- Whipped egg whites

CHIP IN AND BAKE SOME COOKIES

Drop cookies are one of the easiest treats for beginner bakers. They are so fun to bake and share with friends but making the dough is just one part of the work! To advance to the next cookie baking level, you need to know how to prepare your baking pans and finish them off, too.

HOW TO LINE A COOKIE PAN

Parchment paper is a really handy tool for lining cookie and baking pans when you want your treat to lift away neatly. Pull the sheet from the roll and trim a piece the same length as the pan you plan to use. Some cookie bar recipes suggest using a longer piece so you have edges to pull the treats off the pan more easily. If you find the edges keep rolling back up, you can flip the paper over to help keep it flat or fold the edges to form creases.

HOW TO SPACE APART YOUR COOKIES ON A COOKIE PAN

When cookies bake, they often puff up or spread out. It is very important to leave room between them on the cookie pan so that they don't end up all baking into one solid cookie puddle.

Cookie recipes often mention how far apart to space your cookies. We prefer to put only 8 to 12 large cookies or 12 to 15 smaller cookies on a cookie pan at one time, always in a staggered pattern. (See the photo to the left for reference.) Leave at least a two-fingers-width space between each cookie unless the recipe calls for more room.

HOW TO ROTATE COOKIE PANS DURING BAKING

For your treats to bake evenly, it is smart to rotate the pans during baking. Use your oven mitts to pull the pan from the oven, set it on the stovetop, turn it around so that the back faces the front and return it to the oven to finish baking. This helps the baked good brown evenly all across the surface.

If you are baking with two cookie pans at one time, turn the pans back to front but also put the top pan on the lower rack and vice versa. This helps the cookies cook evenly on the top and bottom.

HOW TO COOL COOKIES

Most cookies are really delicate and soft when they first come out of the oven. It's a great idea to let them cool for 2 to 3 minutes before using a spatula to transfer them to a wire rack. This helps the cookies firm up so that they don't break when you move them. The wire rack lets air move around the cookies, which makes them cool evenly and helps the cookies be nice and crispy.

ROCK AND ROLL YOUR DOUGH

Most cookies in this book are drop cookies; that is, spooned onto your cookie pans. Some fancier cookies, such as sugar cookies (page 66) and our favorite gingerbread cutouts (page 159) require rolling out the dough first.

STEP 1: PREP YOUR WORK SPACE

Set out the parchment-lined cookie pans so you have a place to put your freshly cut cookie. Gather the cookie cutters you plan to use and set them near your work space. Find a clean ruler to measure your dough thickness and set it with the cutters.

Place a small cup of all-purpose flour in a small bowl and keep it handy for using throughout the rolling. Set out a large cutting board. Sprinkle a rounded spoonful of flour over the surface and rub it around with your fingers so the dough doesn't stick to it. Rub another spoonful of flour all over your rolling pin.

STEP 2: SHAPE THE DOUGH INTO A FLAT CIRCLE

It's easier to work with smaller portions of dough rather than the entire batch all at once. Divide the dough in half and form a flat-topped circle by gently patting the dough with clean hands. Place it on top of the flour-coated work surface. Be careful to not to handle your dough too much or it will soften.

STEP 3: ROLL THE DOUGH EVENLY

Sprinkle a pinch of flour over the top of the dough and then use your rolling pin to gently but firmly roll out the dough.

Work with shorter strokes to start. First roll away from yourself, then roll from side to side. Keep rotating your direction and always roll from the center out to the sides.

Keep rolling your dough until it is very even and flattened to the correct thickness. You can use your clean ruler to measure and check the thickness of the dough and compare that to what the recipe calls for.

STEP 4: CUT THE DOUGH

Dip your cookie cutters into the bowl of flour near your work space before you cut the dough.

Find a spot close to the outer edge of the rolled dough to place your cutter and then press down firmly. Give the cutter a tiny little wiggle to make sure you cut through the entire dough.

Gently peel back the dough around the outside edge of the cutter and then lift straight up to reveal your cut cookie. You can use your fingers to carefully transfer the shape to your prepared pans or, for extremely delicate shapes, you might want to dip a spatula in the flour and use that to scoop and lift the shape.

Continue to cut the shapes from the outside edges in. You can roll the remaining dough scraps back into a ball and roll it out with your rolling pin to get as many cookies from your dough as possible.

ROLLING PIECRUST

For the Mini Pi Day Pies (page 79) and the Maple-Spiced Pumpkin Pie (page 135), you may need to roll out the piecrust even when using refrigerated pie dough.

For the bottom crust of the pumpkin pie: Prepare a floured cutting board or mat as you would for the drop cookies. Unroll the prepared piecrust and just give it a gentle roll with your rolling pin. This helps smooth out the dough and will give you more edge to crimp.

For the dough scraps from the mini pies or pumpkin pie accents: When you use a cookie cutter on the pie dough, you'll need to reroll the scraps to make the dough last for the entire recipe. Just pinch the scraps together and form a small ball of dough. Lay it on the floured work surface and roll it out as thinly as the original piecrust so that everything bakes evenly.

FUN WITH FROSTING

Here's a little secret: Your friends may or may not notice if you use a boxed cake mix, but making homemade frosting will create a treat that blows their mind. Those store-bought tubs are good in a pinch, but if you only have time to make one thing from scratch? Go for the frosting!

HOW TO PICK THE JUST-RIGHT FROSTING

- **SWEET BUTTERCREAM FROSTING (PAGE 38):** The most classic frosting, perfect for almost anything. Can be easily tinted to a custom color to match your party.

- **CHOCOLATE FUDGE FROSTING (PAGE 41):** Rich and delicious, a perfect base for brightly colored sprinkles or fresh berries.

- **CREAM CHEESE FROSTING (PAGE 42):** If your cake has bananas, carrots or pineapple, this is the frosting you need! It's perfect for just about any cake if you want a little extra zing. We love it with just about anything, but it is especially delicious as a cookie frosting.

HOW TO TINT FROSTING THE PERFECT COLOR

If you want to turn your frosting a special color to match your theme, you'll need food coloring gels or food color drops.

First, decide if you need more than one color of frosting. Be sure to divide the plain white frosting into separate bowls before you tint it, if you need more colors for your design!

If you're tinting the entire batch of frosting, it is easiest to do while it is still in the mixing bowl. Carefully add just one or two drops of color. Mix the frosting on a low speed to combine the color. Be sure to scrape the bowl; don't leave any pockets of untinted frosting.

You can continue to add color one or two drops at a time until you've reached the color that you want. Be careful; you can always add another drop, but you can't take it out. If you're tinting multiple colors in smaller bowls, you can easily blend in the color by hand with a spatula or butter knife.

HOW TO FILL A PASTRY BAG

We usually spread frosting on cakes with a butter knife or spatula, but if you want to pipe it onto a cupcake or add special decorations to your cake, you'll want to use a special pastry bag and piping tip. You can find these at your local craft store in the cake decorating section, or online.

Prepare your pastry bag by cutting off ½ inch (1.3 cm) of the pointy tip. Insert the plastic coupler and gently push it to the bottom of the bag. Place the metal tip you want to use over the plastic bag and coupler and then screw into place with the circular piece of the coupler. Place the bag tip down inside a wide-mouth Mason jar or drinking glass. Fold down the edges of the bag over the edge of the glass.

Scoop a heaping spoonful of frosting and carefully drop it down into the pastry bag. Hold the edges of the bag in place against the glass. Fill your bag just a little more than halfway so you have room to twist the top. Once it is half full, fold the sides of the bag back up and twist the bag closed. Add the frosting to your treat by squeezing from the top down — not in the middle, or the frosting will fly out up through the opening at the top!

A NOTE ON CONSISTENCY

Frosting should always be used at room temperature so it is just the right consistency for spreading and piping. If it is too cold, it will harden and not spread. If it is too hot, it will get soupy and melt.

The heat from your own hands is actually enough to melt frosting if you hold the piping bag for too long. Just be sure to work with one small portion in your pastry bag at a time. It will be easier to keep refilling it a few times from your main bowl of frosting rather than to work with wet frosting that has melted from being held.

SWEET BUTTER-CREAM FROSTING

YIELD: FROSTS 24 CUPCAKES OR ONE 9 X 13-INCH (23 X 33-CM) SHEET CAKE

Buttercream frosting is a deliciously simple recipe that is perfect for any birthday treat, from gorgeous frosted cupcakes to sweet and easy sprinkle-covered cookies. It is a perfect treat topper all year long for anything you have to celebrate. You can match the color to any festive event you have planned, or keep it simple and white to show off your twinkling sprinkles!

1 lb (4 sticks [450 g]) salted butter, softened
4 cups (480 g) powdered sugar
1½ tbsp (23 ml) vanilla extract
Gel food coloring (optional)

Place the butter in your large mixing bowl, and beat it with an electric mixer on medium speed until smooth, about 2 minutes. Add the powdered sugar 1 cup (120 g) at a time, beating it on medium speed until it is mixed into the butter, and scraping the sides of the bowl before adding the next cup.

Once all of the powdered sugar is mixed in, add the vanilla. Stop the mixer to scrape the sides of the bowl and then beat the frosting on medium-high speed until it is light and fluffy, about 2 minutes. Add the food coloring 1 to 2 drops at a time, if desired, until it is evenly mixed throughout.

NOTE: Both buttercream and cream cheese frosting can be made a few days ahead of your party. Store the frosting in an airtight container in the fridge. Set the container on your counter several hours before you plan to spread it on your treat, so it has time to soften up to room temperature.

CHOCOLATE FUDGE FROSTING

YIELD: FROSTS 24 CUPCAKES OR ONE 9-INCH (23-CM) LAYER CAKE

This rich, fudgy frosting is the perfect topping for the Classic Buttery Yellow Cupcakes (page 50) or the Epic Chocolate Layer Cake (page 58). No need to tint it a color; just dress it up with sprinkles, candies, fresh berries or even chopped nuts!

½ lb (2 sticks [225 g]) salted butter, softened
½ cup (55 g) unsweetened cocoa powder
3 to 4 tbsp (45 to 59 ml) milk
5 cups (600 g) powdered sugar
1 tsp vanilla extract

In your large mixing bowl, combine the butter and cocoa powder and mix them with an electric mixer on low speed until just blended. Scrape the bowl.

Measure 3 tablespoons (45 ml) of milk and place it in a small cup with a spout. Set it next to your mixing bowl.

Add the powdered sugar to the butter mixture, 1 cup (120 g) at a time, stirring it in and scraping the bowl before you add the next cup. Once all of the sugar is incorporated, add the vanilla and stir to combine.

Mix the frosting on medium speed while you slowly pour in the 3 tablespoons (45 ml) of milk you set aside. Stop the mixer to scrape the sides of the bowl before you continue to beat the frosting on medium speed until it is light and fluffy, about 2 to 3 minutes.

If the frosting is still too thick, you can add the remaining 1 tablespoon (15 ml) of milk and beat it in on medium speed.

CREAM CHEESE FROSTING

YIELD: FROSTS ONE 8-INCH (20.5-CM) SINGLE LAYER CAKE OR 12 CUPCAKES

This is the Easter Bunny's favorite frosting for sure. A carrot cake or the Hummingbird Cupcakes (page 97) just wouldn't be the same without it! Even though it is a springtime classic, you can top treats with it all year long. Try spreading some on the Gingerbread Cookie Cutouts (page 159) for a festive wintery twist.

8 oz (225 g) cream cheese, softened

8 tbsp (1 stick [112 g]) salted butter, softened

½ tsp vanilla extract

2 cups (240 g) powdered sugar

In your large mixing bowl, combine the softened cream cheese and butter. Beat them with an electric mixer on medium speed until combined and smooth, about 2 minutes. You shouldn't see any lumps of cream cheese or butter.

Add the vanilla and powdered sugar and mix on low speed until just combined, 1 to 2 minutes. Stop the mixer to scrape the bowl and then increase the speed to medium-high and beat until light and fluffy, 2 to 3 minutes.

NOTE: Both buttercream and cream cheese frosting can be made a few days ahead of your party. Store the frosting in an airtight container in the fridge. Set the container on your counter several hours before you plan to spread it on your treat, so it has time to soften up to room temperature.

CUSTOMIZE YOUR OWN COOKIE GLAZE

YIELD: FROSTS 24 COOKIES

These handy glazes help sprinkles stick to your sugar cookies, but can also be used on top of other simple pastries. Here are three flavors you can use to get you started!

BASIC VANILLA COOKIE GLAZE
2¼ cups (270 g) powdered sugar
2 tbsp (30 ml) light corn syrup
1 tsp vanilla extract
1 to 2 tbsp (15 to 30 ml) milk
Gel food coloring (optional)

PEPPERMINT GLAZE
Substitute ¼ tsp peppermint extract to replace the vanilla

MAPLE GLAZE
Substitute 1 tsp maple syrup to replace the vanilla

In a medium bowl, combine the powdered sugar and corn syrup. Measure your flavor extract of choice and add it to the bowl. Add 1 tablespoon (15 ml) of milk and then mix everything together with a fork.

If the glaze is too thick, add more milk, 1 teaspoon at a time. The glaze should feel like a very thick syrup. Add a drop or two of food coloring, if you'd like, and stir it in. This glaze is runny but thick. It is best for spooning onto your cookies. It will dry smooth and firm once completely set.

SWEET AND SMOOTH STRAWBERRY JAM SAUCE

We love to use this simple strawberry jam all year long for everything from PB&J to drizzling over pancakes. Thinner and smoother than traditional jams you can buy at the store, this recipe is easy to stir into frosting, use as a cake filling, top the drop biscuits (page 98) with it or swirl it into Strawberry Pretzel Cheesecake Bars (page 140). Make a batch (or two!) when strawberries are fresh in season where you live and it will taste like spring every month of the year.

2 qt (1.4 kg) fresh strawberries

4 cups (800 g) sugar

¾ cup (177 ml) water

1 (1.75-oz [49-g]) box Sure-Jell Original fruit pectin, or 5 tbsp (75 g) powdered pectin

Wash and completely dry six 1-cup (237-ml) Mason jars with lids or other similar freezer-safe containers that you will use to hold your jam. Really thoroughly wash and drain the strawberries. Use a butter knife to cut off the leafy tops and stems and discard them. Put the strawberries in a large bowl and use a potato masher to crush the berries. Any lumps you see in the bowl will remain in the jam, so mash them as much as you need for the jam consistency you prefer.

Measure exactly 2 cups (340 g) of mashed berries and place them in a clean mixing bowl. Stir in the sugar and let it stand for 10 minutes, stirring once in a while to combine the fruit juices.

Have a timer ready to go for this next step. Set your strawberry bowl next to the stovetop. Place the water in a small saucepan and add the pectin. Stir them to combine and then place the pan over high heat. While stirring constantly, bring the pectin mixture to a boil. When you see large bubbles, set your timer and boil the pectin for 1 more minute, then remove from the heat.

Carefully pour the pectin mixture into the strawberries, using a spatula to scrape the pan and get everything along the sides and bottom of the pan. You may want to ask an adult to help you with this step.

Set your timer again and stir the pectin and fruit together for 3 minutes, or until the sugar is mostly dissolved.

Use a clean spoon to fill your freezer-safe containers with the jam while it is still warm. Leave a ½-inch (1.3-cm) space between the top of the jam and the top of the container; it will expand once it is frozen. Be sure to wipe the outside of the jar with a clean, damp paper towel, then immediately cover each container with the lids. Let them stand at room temperature for 24 hours.

Store the jam in the freezer for up to 12 months. When you want to use it, thaw it overnight in the fridge. It will keep in the fridge for up to 3 weeks.

DECORATE YOUR CAKES LIKE A BOSS

TO FROST A SHEET CAKE

Drop the frosting in large spoonfuls all over the top of your completely cooled cake, not just in one heap.

Use a butter knife to spread the frosting evenly over the top. Be careful that you don't nick or scrape the top of your cake with the knife, or it will mix crumbs into the frosting. Keep the knife parallel to the cake, and just continue to spread and work the frosting until every spot has been covered.

Use the knife to make a pretty swirling pattern over the top for the finishing touch.

TO FROST A CUPCAKE

You can spread the frosting on with a butter knife, like you would for a regular cake, or you can pipe it on using a pastry bag with a large open decorating tip (see page 37).

Pipe the frosting in a circular motion, starting in the center and working your way out, to completely cover the cupcake. Keep swirling the frosting until the entire surface is covered.

ADDING SPRINKLES

Always be sure to add your sprinkles while the frosting is still fresh. Once it has dried, which can only take a few minutes, the sprinkles will bounce off and not stick.

FOR A GIFT WRAP DESIGN ON A CAKE

To make the fun design shown on the right (see page 57 for the recipe), scoop 1 cup (256 g) of frosting into a separate bowl, and tint it the color you desire. Spoon it into a prepared pastry bag (see page 37) and twist the top closed. Set the pastry bag to the side. Then, spread an even layer of white frosting over the top of the cake.

Next, use your tinted frosting to pipe two long lines across the cake to form the ribbon. Squeeze two loops and two tails to form the bow where the ribbons meet. If you still have tinted frosting left, you can use it to squeeze round polka dots over the top of the "gift wrap" or write a message.

TO FROST A LAYER CAKE

See the recipe for Epic Chocolate Layer Cake (page 58) for detailed instructions and photos.

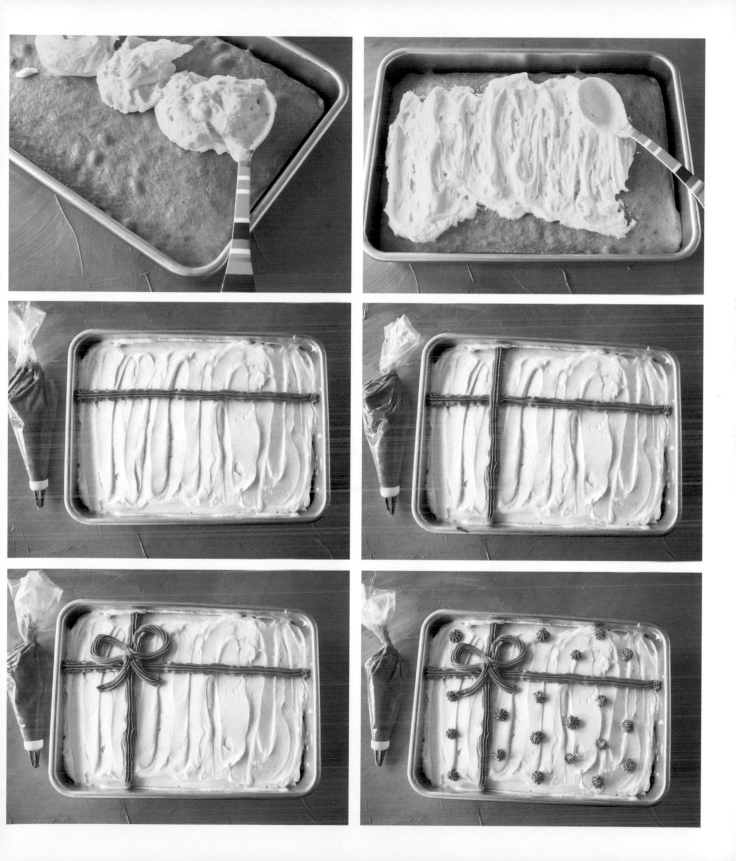

Sprinkle PARTY TIME

Whether you're celebrating a birthday or something else spectacular, nothing says "Let's party!" like a sprinkle-topped treat made with love. Those rainbow-colored festive sprinkles look just like edible confetti and spread joy to everyone who sees them.

When you want to bake up a magnificent treat for someone special, all you need to do is simply choose your own adventure:

Will it be a cupcake, a cookie or a donut?

Do you want frosting, cookie glaze or whipped cream?

Which color do you want to make your treat?

Then, top it off with the just-right sprinkles to give it a magic finishing touch!

Mix and match your favorite combinations by choosing between our Classic Buttery Yellow Cupcakes (page 50) or Confetti Cupcake Cuties (page 53) with sweet vanilla buttercream or tangy cream cheese frostings. Maybe you want to spoil your very important person (VIP) with a sprinkle-topped birthday donut (page 69) or a Custom Color Cookie Bar (page 65).

All the building blocks you need to create stunning tasty birthday masterpieces are right here.

CLASSIC BUTTERY YELLOW CUPCAKES

YIELD:
12 CUPCAKES

A birthday party essential—who doesn't love a light and fluffy yellow cake? These sweet vanilla cupcakes are so much better than any box mix you've tried; you won't believe how easy they are to make by yourself. Top them with a sweet vanilla buttercream frosting and dress them up with sprinkles for a perfectly pretty party treat.

1½ cups (188 g) all-purpose flour

1 cup (200 g) sugar

1½ tsp (7 g) baking powder

½ tsp salt

3 large eggs

8 tbsp (1 stick [112 g]) salted butter, softened

½ cup (115 g) sour cream

1½ tsp (8 ml) vanilla extract

1 batch Sweet Buttercream Frosting (page 38)

Sprinkles, for decorating

Preheat the oven to 350°F (175°C, or gas mark 4). Line each well of a 12-muffin tin with a double layer of cupcake wrappers and set aside.

In your large mixing bowl, combine the flour, sugar, baking powder and salt. Whisk them together.

In a small bowl, separate the egg yolks from two of the eggs and discard the whites. Add the entire third egg and check for shells. Cut the softened butter into eight pieces so that it mixes more easily. Spoon the sour cream into a ½-cup (118-ml) measuring cup. Fill it up completely and then use a knife to level it off so you have just the right amount. Add the eggs, butter, sour cream and vanilla to the mixing bowl that contains the flour.

Beat everything together with an electric mixer on medium-low speed until just combined, about 20 seconds. Stop the mixer and scrape down the bowl. Beat the batter on medium speed until it is smooth, about 30 seconds. Scrape the bowl again to check for any dry pockets of flour. The batter will be quite thick.

Spoon the batter evenly among the prepared muffin wells. Each one will be two-thirds full. Bake for 10 minutes and then quickly rotate the pan in the oven. Bake for another 8 to 10 minutes, or until the tops are light golden brown and a toothpick inserted into the center of a cupcake comes out clean.

Remove from the oven and let the cupcakes cool right in the muffin tin for 15 minutes. Carefully transfer them to a wire rack to cool the rest of the way. Once the cupcakes are completely cooled, simply spread frosting on them with a butter knife or pipe frosting however you prefer. To match our design, use a tiny heart-shaped cookie cutter to do the sprinkle trick from page 23.

SPRINKLES

CONFETTI CUPCAKE CUTIES

**YIELD:
24 CUPCAKES**

What's better than sprinkles on a cupcake? How about sprinkles *inside* a cupcake?! These pretty little cakes have a party in every bite.

2½ cups (313 g) all-purpose flour
1⅓ cups (267 g) sugar
1 tsp baking soda
1 tsp salt
2 large eggs
1½ cups (355 ml) buttermilk
1 cup (237 ml) vegetable oil
1 tsp vanilla extract
½ cup (80 g) sprinkles, plus more for decorating
1 batch Sweet Buttercream Frosting (page 38)

Preheat the oven to 350°F (175°C, or gas mark 4). Line each well of two 12-muffin tins with a double layer of cupcake wrappers and set aside.

In your large mixing bowl, combine the flour, sugar, baking soda and salt. Whisk them together.

In a small bowl, separate the egg whites from the yolks and discard the yolks.

In a medium bowl, combine the buttermilk, vegetable oil, egg whites and vanilla and stir them together.

Add the wet buttermilk mixture to the flour mixture and mix together with an electric mixer on low speed until combined, about 2 minutes. Stop the mixer and scrape down the bowl and check for any dry flour pockets. Scrape the beaters. Add the sprinkles to the batter and fold them in with a spatula.

Spoon the batter evenly among the prepared muffin wells. Each well should be about two-thirds full. Bake for 16 to 20 minutes, or until the tops are lightly golden and a toothpick inserted into the center of a cupcake comes out clean.

Remove from the oven and let the cupcakes cool in the muffin tins for 5 minutes. Carefully transfer them to a wire rack to completely cool before frosting.

To decorate the cupcakes as shown, use any open star-shaped frosting tip you have. We like size 32 or 1M by Wilton. Pipe the frosting in a circle starting at the outside edge and circling in towards the center. Shake or pinch the sprinkles over the cupcakes with your fingers.

GIANT BIRTHDAY COOKIE CAKE

**YIELD:
8 TO 10 SERVINGS**

The easiest birthday treat to take on the go is a giant cookie cake. Whereas cupcakes and cakes may topple over, this perfectly portable cookie treat is great when you need to bring it to a friend. Mix and match the colorful sprinkles with their favorite colors.

Baking spray, for pan
8 tbsp (1 stick [112 g]) salted butter, softened
¾ cup (150 g) sugar
1 large egg
2 tsp (10 ml) vanilla extract
1¼ cups (156 g) all-purpose flour
¼ tsp salt
½ tsp baking soda
1 tsp cornstarch
⅔ cup (117 g) white chocolate chips, plus more for decoration
½ cup (80 g) rainbow sprinkles, plus more for decoration
½ batch frosting (pages 38–42) (optional)
Chocolate candies, for decorating (optional)

Preheat the oven to 350°F (175°C, or gas mark 4). Spray a 9-inch (23-cm) pie plate with baking spray and set aside.

In your large mixing bowl, combine the butter and sugar. Beat them together with an electric mixer on medium speed until light and fluffy. Stop the mixer and scrape the bowl.

Crack the egg into a small bowl to check for shells. Add the egg and vanilla to the butter mixture and beat on medium speed until just combined. Scrape the bowl.

In a medium bowl, combine the flour, salt, baking soda and cornstarch. Whisk them together. Add the flour mixture to the butter mixture and beat them together until just combined.

Scrape the beaters and the bowl and add the chocolate chips and sprinkles. Stir them in by hand, using a spoon. Press the dough into the prepared pie plate. Sprinkle a small handful of chocolate chips and sprinkles over the top and gently press them into the surface.

Bake for 20 to 25 minutes, or until the cookie cake is golden brown and a toothpick inserted in the center comes out clean. Remove from the oven and let cool in the pan.

Once your cookie cake has completely cooled, you can decorate it. Although the cookie is pretty all on its own, you can decorate the edges with a half-batch of one of the frostings from pages 38–42, if desired. We piped frosting flowers with Wilton tip 2D around the edge and dotted each flower with a colorful chocolate candy.

THE BEST BIRTHDAY CAKE FOR THE ONE WHO BAKES FOR YOU

**YIELD:
9 TO 12 SERVINGS**

Where do your birthday cakes come from? It is likely the same person makes sure you have one every year.

This year, turn the tables and make a sheet cake just for them on their birthday! This gift-wrapped cake can be customized in their favorite color and has a special twist adults just love—a hint of almond flavor. Hold off on the sprinkles just this once; they'll love the crunch of the chocolate chips on top instead. Or you can decorate it like our gift wrap design on page 46.

Baking spray, for pan

8 tbsp (1 stick [112 g]) salted butter, softened

1¾ cups (350 g) sugar

4 large eggs

1 tsp vanilla extract

1 tsp almond extract

2⅔ cups (240 g) cake flour (check the substitutions on page 183 if you don't have it!)

2 tsp (9 g) baking powder

½ tsp salt

1½ cups (355 ml) heavy whipping cream

1 cup (175 g) mini chocolate chips

FROSTING

1 batch Sweet Buttercream Frosting (page 38) mixed with 1 tsp almond extract (optional)

Preheat the oven to 350°F (175°C, or gas mark 4). Spray a 9 x 13-inch (23 x 33-cm) baking pan with baking spray and set it aside.

In a large bowl, combine the butter and sugar and beat them together with an electric mixer on medium-high speed until light and fluffy, about 2 minutes. Stop the mixer and scrape the bowl. Crack the eggs into a small bowl to check for shells and then add them to the butter mixture. Mix on medium speed until just combined, about 20 seconds. Scrape the sides of the bowl. Then add the vanilla and almond extracts and stir them in.

In a medium bowl, combine the flour, baking powder and salt and whisk them together. Pour about HALF the flour mixture into the butter mixture and mix them together on medium speed until the flour is all mixed in. Scrape the bowl.

Pour the cream into the batter and mix together until just combined. Add the remaining flour mixture and beat to combine. Scrape down the bowl and then stir in the chocolate chips with a spatula. Pour the cake batter into the prepared baking pan and use a spatula to spread it evenly.

Bake the cake for 35 to 40 minutes, or until a toothpick inserted into the center comes out clean. Remove from the oven and let the cake completely cool in its pan before frosting.

*See photo of the whole cake in "Baking School" on page 47.

EPIC CHOCOLATE LAYER CAKE

YIELD: 10 TO 12 SERVINGS

Once you've mastered the art of the cupcake and can make a sheet cake in your sleep, you're ready to conquer the mother of all birthday cakes—a double-layer chocolate fudge masterpiece. The truth is, a layer cake isn't that much more difficult to bake; it's all in the assembly. The foolproof darkly colored frosting helps you sneakily hide any little happy accidents you might encounter. But when in doubt? Just add sprinkles or pretty fresh berries and everyone will be amazed at your achievement.

2 tbsp (28 g) salted butter, softened, for pans

1¾ cups (219 g) all-purpose flour, plus 2 tbsp (16 g) for pans

2 cups (400 g) sugar

¾ cup (83 g) unsweetened cocoa powder

1½ tsp (7 g) baking powder

1½ tsp (7 g) baking soda

1 tsp salt

1 cup (237 ml) water

1 cup (237 ml) buttermilk

½ cup (118 ml) vegetable oil

2 tsp (10 ml) vanilla extract

2 large eggs

1 batch Chocolate Fudge Frosting (page 41)

Preheat the oven to 350°F (175°C, or gas mark 4).

A layer cake's success starts with prepping your pans. Do not skip the next few steps! This helps ensure you can easily get your layers out of the pans to build your cake.

Trace two 9-inch (23-cm) pans on a large piece of parchment paper. Cut out the circles and set them aside. Place 1 tablespoon (14 g) of the butter in the bottom of each pan. Use your fingers to spread the butter all over the bottom and inside walls of both pans. While your fingers are still coated in butter, place 1 parchment circle at the bottom of each pan. Rub some of the butter over the parchment and smooth out any air bubbles. Wash and dry your hands.

Place 1 tablespoon (8 g) of flour in the bottom of each pan. Over your kitchen sink, gently shake and wiggle the pan to coat the bottom and inside walls of the pan with the flour. Once the entire inside of the pan is dusted with flour, gently turn the pan upside down over the sink and tap the edge against the sink to shake out any excess flour. Set your pans aside while you prepare the batter.

(continued)

Flip the cake layers out of the pans onto a plate (before flip).

Flip the cake layers out of the pans onto a plate (after flip).

Tuck parchment paper under the bottom layer and frost it.

Place the second layer carefully on top.

EPIC CHOCOLATE LAYER CAKE (CONTINUED)

In a medium bowl, combine the sugar, flour, cocoa powder, baking powder, baking soda and salt. Whisk them together and set the bowl aside.

Place the water in a microwave-safe measuring cup and heat in a microwave on HIGH for 3 minutes, or until it is boiling. Use oven mitts to remove the cup and set it on the counter.

In your large mixing bowl, combine the buttermilk, vegetable oil and vanilla. Crack the eggs into a small bowl and check for shells. Add the eggs to the milk mixture. Beat with an electric mixer on medium speed until just combined. Scrape the bowl.

Add the flour mixture to the buttermilk mixture and beat them together on medium speed for 2 minutes. Scrape the bowl.

Carefully pour the hot water into the mixing bowl and mix on low speed to combine. Scrape the bowl. The batter will be very thin. Pour half of the batter into each of your two prepared pans.

Bake for 30 to 35 minutes, or until a toothpick inserted in the center comes out clean. Remove from the oven and let the cakes cool completely before you try to assemble the cake.

TO ASSEMBLE THE CAKE

Use the pictures on the left to help you with these next steps. Set out the cake plate you plan to use to serve your cake. Make sure it is at least 2 inches (5 cm) wider than the cake pans on all sides. Also set out two dinner plates larger than the cake pans.

Take a butter knife and slowly run it around the inside of the cooled cake pans to separate the cake from the pan, trying not to cut into the cake as you go.

Choose which cake you want to form the bottom layer. Pick the one that might be thicker than the other if they aren't perfectly even.

Cover the cake pan with one of the dinner plates, or you can flip it directly onto the cake plate. Using both hands, pinch the plate to the cake pan and quickly flip them over so that the cake is upside down on the plate, but don't pull away the pan just yet! Gently tap and wiggle the cake pan bottom. The parchment paper will release and the cake layer should drop onto the plate.

Gently peel back the parchment paper and throw it away. Now use your hands to carefully and gently pick up the cake layer and turn it right side up. Place it in the center of your pretty cake plate.

Cut several 4-inch (10-cm)-wide strips of waxed or parchment paper. Gently tuck them just under the bottom edge of the cake. This will help keep your cake plate clean from crumbs and frosting splatters and will make the final presentation more pretty.

Spoon several dollops of frosting onto the top of the cake layer. Spread it evenly over the top with a butter knife. Be careful to not poke the cake with your knife. If your cake layer has a dome or rounded top, just add a bit more frosting around the edges to make it even.

Now, flip the second cake layer out onto a dinner plate, using the same method. Peel back the parchment paper and throw it away. Pick up the cake layer and slowly flip it right side up and place it on top of the frosted bottom layer.

Put several spoonfuls of frosting on top of the cake.

Pull the frosting down around the sides and scrape it evenly.

Continue until the sides, then the top, are evenly covered, then smooth it out.

Use your butter knife to make pretty swirls. You did it!

EPIC CHOCOLATE LAYER CAKE (CONTINUED)

TO FROST THE CAKE

If there is a big gap around the edges between your two cake layers, carefully spoon in frosting to fill the holes. If there's no gap, then start with the top of the cake.

Place big spoonfuls of frosting on the top of the cake around the edges. You will frost the sides from the top down. Use a butter knife to make short, gentle strokes to pull the frosting down over the sides. Work in small sections and coat one area of the side at a time. Add more spoons of frosting to the top as needed and rotate the cake to work all around.

Once the sides are covered with frosting, hold the flat edge of your knife parallel to the side of the cake and gently scrape all around the edges to even out the frosting. If you find that there are too many cake crumbs mixed into the frosting, add a thin second layer of frosting to cover them up.

To frost the top of the cake, add a few more spoonfuls of frosting to the top and smooth it out over the entire surface of the cake.

Once the entire cake is covered with frosting, use the flat tip of your butter knife to make short, small circular swirls all over the top and sides of the cake. This will give your cake a simple pretty finish and helps to hide any spots that need it.

Sprinkle your sprinkles over the top of the cake or decorate with a border of fresh berries.

Gently remove the paper strips and use a clean paper towel to wipe up any messes along the edge of the cake plate.

CUSTOM COLOR COOKIE BARS

**YIELD:
18 COOKIE BARS**

Does your best friend have a favorite color? Maybe you want to celebrate your favorite team or show your school pride. For any special occasion you can imagine, you can make personalized cookie bars that match the colors you want! You can find seasonal color blends in the holiday department at the grocery store or stop by a local candy shop to mix and match your own. These superdelicious bars really give you something to sink your teeth into!

Baking spray, for pan

½ lb (2 sticks [225 g]) salted butter, melted

2 large eggs

2 tsp (10 ml) vanilla extract

2 cups (450 g) packed light brown sugar

2½ cups (313 g) all-purpose flour

1½ tsp (7 g) baking powder

1 tsp salt

1½ cups (300 g) colored chocolate candies (M&M's, Reese's Pieces, etc.), divided

1 cup (175 g) mini chocolate chips, divided

Preheat the oven to 350°F (175°C, or gas mark 4). Line the bottom and sides of a 9 x 13–inch (23 x 33–cm) baking pan with a large piece of aluminum foil for easy removal of the cookie bars. Spray the foil with baking spray and set aside.

Place the butter in a microwave-safe bowl. Heat on HIGH for 40 seconds to melt it. Use oven mitts to remove the bowl and carefully stir the butter. Continue to heat for 15-second intervals until it is completely melted and smooth. Set it aside to cool a little bit.

Crack the eggs into your large mixing bowl and check for shells. Then, add the vanilla. Use a fork to beat the egg mixture until it is a smooth yellow color. Add the brown sugar and stir to combine. Gently pour in the melted butter and stir to combine.

Add the flour, baking powder and salt to the bowl and stir together until just combined with the egg mixture. Add HALF of the chocolate candies and HALF of the chocolate chips to the bowl and fold them in by hand, using a spoon.

Put the cookie dough in your prepared baking pan and use a spoon or clean hands to spread it as evenly as you can. The dough will be very thick and sticky, so just work slowly and take your time.

Sprinkle the remaining candies and chocolate chips over the top of the dough and gently press them into the top. This will help the colors show right on top!

Bake for 35 to 40 minutes. It should be golden brown and firmly set. Remove from the oven and let it cool before you remove the baked slab by pulling up the edges of the aluminum foil. Cut into rectangular bars for serving.

SIMPLY SWEET SUGAR COOKIES

YIELD: 3 DOZEN COOKIES (CUT WITH A MEDIUM COOKIE CUTTER)

These sugar cookies are the perfect blank canvas for your creative designs. You can decorate them to match any season or celebration during the year. Try them with one of the simple glaze recipes (page 43) or spread your favorite frosting over them and top with sprinkles for a special treat your family will love.

½ lb (2 sticks [225 g]) salted butter, softened

1 cup (200 g) sugar

1 large egg

1 tsp vanilla extract

½ tsp almond extract

3 cups (475 g) all-purpose flour, plus more for dusting

2 tsp (9 g) baking powder

½ tsp salt

Preheat the oven to 350°F (175°C, or gas mark 4). Set out two cookie pans and line them with parchment paper; set aside.

In your large mixing bowl, combine the butter and sugar and beat with an electric mixer on medium-high speed until light and fluffy. Crack the egg into a small bowl to check for shells. Add the egg and extracts to the butter mixture and beat to combine.

In a medium bowl, combine the flour, baking powder and salt and whisk them together. Add the flour mixture to the butter and beat on medium-low speed until the dough comes together.

If the dough is too thick for your mixer to work, scrape everything off the beaters onto a floured work surface. Rub some flour on your clean hands and knead the dough into one solid portion. Pat the dough into a flat disk and sprinkle it with flour. Use a rolling pin to roll out the dough so that it is evenly ¼ inch (6 mm) thick.

Dip your cookie cutters in flour and cut out your shapes. Knead the remaining dough scraps back into a disk and repeat the rolling and cutting until you've made as many cookies as you can. Place the cookies on the prepared pans with a little bit of space between them so you don't overcrowd the pan.

Bake for 6 to 8 minutes. The cookies should not brown around the edges. Remove from the oven and let the cookies cool on the pans for 3 to 5 minutes before transferring to a wire rack. Once cool, frost with cookie glaze (page 43) or frosting (pages 38–42).

I
L ♥ V E
YOU

BIRTHDAY SPRINKLE DONUTS

**YIELD:
8 DONUTS**

When you just can't wait for dessert to have your birthday cake, why not wake up to a batch of birthday donuts? You can make these the night before the big day. If someone in your family has a birthday, why not surprise them with breakfast in bed? Don't forget a glass of milk!

Baking spray, for pans
1 cup (125 g) all-purpose flour
1 tsp baking powder
¼ tsp baking soda
¼ tsp salt
¼ tsp ground nutmeg
¼ cup (50 g) granulated sugar
1 tbsp (15 g) light brown sugar
1 large egg
¼ cup (59 ml) milk

¼ cup (60 g) plain Greek yogurt
2 tbsp (28 g) salted butter, melted
1½ tsp (8 ml) vanilla extract
¼ cup (40 g) rainbow sprinkles

GLAZE
¼ cup (59 ml) milk
2 cups (240 g) powdered sugar
1 tsp vanilla extract

Extra sprinkles, for decoration

Preheat the oven to 350°F (175°C, or gas mark 4). Spray the wells of two donut pans with baking spray and set aside.

In your large mixing bowl, combine the flour, baking powder, baking soda, salt, nutmeg, granulated sugar and brown sugar and whisk them together. Set the bowl aside.

Crack the egg into a medium bowl and check for shells. Add the milk, yogurt, butter and vanilla and whisk together until smooth.

Slowly pour the milk mixture into the flour mixture and stir them together until just combined. Gently fold in the sprinkles, being careful to not overstir them or the colors may bleed.

Pour the batter into a large resealable plastic bag and seal it closed. Use scissors to snip the corner off the bag and pipe the batter into the prepared donut wells. Fill each well about three-quarters full. Bake for 8 to 10 minutes, or until the edges are golden. Remove from the oven and let the donuts cool in the pan for 5 minutes, then transfer to a wire rack.

While the donuts are baking and cooling, prepare the glaze. In a large bowl, combine the milk, powdered sugar and vanilla. Whisk them together until the sugar has dissolved and the glaze is smooth.

Lay a large piece of waxed or parchment paper on the counter. Place the wire rack of donuts over the paper. Carefully dip the top of a donut in the glaze and place it, glaze side up, on the rack. Immediately, while the glaze is still wet, sprinkle the sprinkles over the top and then repeat with the remaining donuts. If the glaze gets too thick, you can add a small splash of milk and stir to thin it out.

BIRTHDAY CAKE POPCORN

**YIELD:
12 SERVINGS**

Nothing says "party time" like sprinkle-covered popcorn! This delicious treat is a clever idea for a movie-themed birthday party or for a just-because party snack. It looks simply adorable bundled into clear gift bags tied with a bow for thank you gifts, too. Just as with the Custom Color Cookie Bars (page 65), you can mix and match the candies and sprinkles to match your party perfectly!

24 cups (240 g) prepared plain popcorn, or 2 batches homemade popcorn made from ½ cup (96 g) kernels

3 cups (525 g) white chocolate chips

3 heaping tbsp (52 g) yellow cake mix (just the powdered mix, don't prepare the cake batter)

1 (11.4-oz [324-g]) bag M&M's

Sprinkles

Place the popcorn in a very large mixing bowl.

Place the white chocolate chips in a microwave-safe bowl. Heat on HIGH for 30 seconds and then use oven mitts to remove the bowl. Stir the chips and then continue to heat in 15-second intervals until the chocolate is melted. When the chocolate is nice and smooth, stir in the cake mix.

Pour the chocolate mixture over the popcorn and use a large cooking spoon to stir the popcorn and coat it with the chocolate.

Spread out the popcorn onto a large sheet of waxed or parchment paper. To avoid having the candy colors run everywhere, be sure to let the popcorn cool for 2 to 3 minutes. Don't wait too long though, or the sprinkles may not stick. Sprinkle the candies and sprinkles evenly over the popcorn. Let the mixture completely cool and harden. Break the popcorn into large pieces and serve in party cups.

SPRINKLE-DIPPED CRISPY TREATS

**YIELD:
12 TREATS**

If you want to surprise a friend with a birthday treat but don't need an entire cake, this treat's for you! You can make these dainty yummies in advance of the special day in just a pinch.

Baking spray, for pan and spoon
3 tbsp (42 g) salted butter
1 (10-oz [280-g]) package mini marshmallows
6 cups (126 g) crisped rice cereal
12 oz (340 g) candy melts
Sprinkles, for decoration

Spray a 9 x 13-inch (23 x 33–cm) baking pan with baking spray and set aside.

Find a microwave-safe bowl that is large enough to fit all the cereal with room for messy stirring. Add the butter and marshmallows to the bowl and place it in the microwave. Heat on HIGH for 2 minutes. Use oven mitts to remove the bowl and stir the butter together with the marshmallows. If necessary, heat for 1 additional minute and keep stirring until the marshmallows are smooth.

Pour the cereal into the marshmallow mixture and stir to combine. Carefully pour the mixture into your prepared baking pan and spread evenly. Spray a cooking spoon with baking spray and gently pack in the cereal with the back of the spoon. Let the treats cool completely.

Once cooled, cut the treats into squares, using a butter knife. Place the pan next to a large piece of waxed paper on your counter; this will become your work station.

Place the candy melts in a medium microwave-safe bowl. Heat on HIGH for 30 seconds and stir. Heat for 15 seconds and vigorously stir the candy to smooth it out. Heat it in 15-second intervals until the candy is completely melted and smooth.

Carefully dip half of each treat into the melted candy. Let the excess candy drip off back into the bowl before placing it on the waxed paper. As the candy starts to cool, it will begin to get very thick. You can use a spoon or butter knife to spread the candy over the top or sides of each treat if dipping becomes too difficult.

Decorate with sprinkles while the candy coating is still soft. Let the treats set completely before serving, about 15 minutes.

NOTE: You can carefully insert paper straws or candy sticks to turn your treats into pops. If this is your plan, be sure to cut your treats into small pieces so they don't get too top-heavy for the sticks.

Spring
PARTIES

Spring is simply bursting with colorful things to celebrate. Love and laughter are the themes of the season. Now is a great time to bake up a joyful surprise for the people you care about most.

Bring the beauty of nature in and set a pretty Easter table covered in our Dainty Daisy Cupcakes (page 89) or whimsical Bird's Nest Haystack Cookies (page 86). Don't miss the delectable Hummingbird Cupcakes (page 97); your mom will love them!

You'll find that spring flavors are light and bright. From the fresh and delicious Carrot Cake Donuts with Cream Cheese Glaze (page 93) to the Tropical Lime Cookies (page 94), we have all kinds of fun new treats for you to try.

Want something with a little more richness? Your favorite sweeties are sure to adore the deeply fudgy Chocolate-Covered Strawberry Brownies (page 76) for Valentine's Day or the decadent homemade mint-chocolate pudding cups (page 85) for Earth Day, too!

CHOCOLATE-COVERED STRAWBERRY BROWNIES

YIELD: 12 BROWNIES

These rich and fudgy brownies are superdelicious all on their own, but when you top them with a sweet strawberry frosting and a creamy chocolate topping, you have a chocolate-covered strawberry treat your family will simply love for Valentine's Day. The pretty peek-a-boo filling is just right for making their hearts flutter.

BROWNIES

Baking spray, for pan

½ cup (88 g) semisweet chocolate chips

10 tbsp (1 stick plus 2 tbsp [140 g]) salted butter

1 cup (200 g) sugar

2 tsp (10 ml) vanilla extract

2 large eggs

¾ cup (90 g) all-purpose flour

¼ cup (28 g) unsweetened cocoa powder

½ tsp salt

PREPARE THE BROWNIES

Preheat the oven to 350°F (175°C, or gas mark 4). Spray a 9 x 13–inch (23 x 33–cm) baking pan with baking spray and set aside.

In a large, microwave-safe mixing bowl, combine the chocolate chips and butter. Heat them on HIGH for 1 minute and use oven mitts to remove the bowl. Stir them together and continue to heat in 15-second increments until completely melted and smooth.

Add the sugar and vanilla to the bowl and whisk them together. Crack the eggs into a small bowl and check for shells. Whisk them into the chocolate mixture. Add the flour, cocoa powder and salt to the bowl and use a spatula to stir them together. Pour the batter into your prepared pan and use the spatula to spread it out evenly.

Bake for 30 minutes, or until a toothpick inserted into the center comes out clean. Remove from the oven and let cool completely in the pan.

(continued)

CHOCOLATE-COVERED STRAWBERRY BROWNIES (CONTINUED)

STRAWBERRY FILLING

8 tbsp (1 stick [112 g]) salted butter, softened

1 cup (120 g) powdered sugar

¼ cup (59 ml) Sweet and Smooth Strawberry Jam Sauce (page 44)

CHOCOLATE TOPPING

1 (10-oz [280-g]) package semisweet chocolate chips

8 tbsp (1 stick [112 g]) salted butter

PREPARE THE STRAWBERRY FILLING

Place the butter in your large mixing bowl and add the powdered sugar. Beat them together with an electric mixer on medium-high speed until they are smooth. Stop the mixer and scrape the bowl. Add the strawberry jam and beat them together until combined, about 30 seconds.

Spread the strawberry filling over the top of the completely cooled brownies. If they are still warm, the filling will melt and get runny. Cover the brownies with aluminum foil and chill in the refrigerator until the filling is completely set, 30 minutes to 1 hour.

PREPARE THE CHOCOLATE TOPPING

Place the chocolate chips in a microwave-safe bowl. Use a butter knife to cut the butter into 8 smaller pieces and add them to the bowl. Microwave for 1 minute on HIGH and then use oven mitts to remove the bowl. Stir the chocolate and butter together. Continue to heat in 15-second intervals, stirring each time, until the chocolate is completely melted and smooth. Set the bowl on your counter and let the chocolate cool for 10 minutes.

Remove the brownies from the fridge, remove the foil cover and gently pour the chocolate over the top of the brownies. Use a spatula to spread it evenly. Cover the brownies again and place back in the fridge to cool and set.

To serve, use a butter knife to cut the brownies into squares. Be sure to store the brownies in the fridge, covered; they'll last for up to 1 week.

MINI PI DAY PIES

**YIELD:
24 MINI PIES**

What's the most delicious way to celebrate math? Pi Day, of course! On March 14 (3/14), celebrate all things pi (3.14159. . .) with—what else—miniature pies! These adorable tiny versions of all-American apple and cherry pies would also be simply perfect for the Fourth of July this summer.

2 boxes (4 crusts) refrigerated piecrust

All-purpose flour, for dusting

APPLE PIE FILLING

2½ cups (313 g) peeled and chopped apples

¼ cup (50 g) granulated sugar

2 tbsp (16 g) all-purpose flour

1 tsp ground cinnamon

1 tsp vanilla extract

⅛ tsp ground nutmeg

CHERRY PIE FILLING

1 (21-oz [595-g]) can cherry pie filling

½ tsp almond extract

(continued)

MINI PI DAY PIES (CONTINUED)

Preheat the oven to 425°F (220°C, or gas mark 7). Set out a 12-well muffin tin. We'll be baking one flavor of mini pies at a time. Set out one box of piecrust dough (two piecrusts' worth) on the counter so that they can warm up a bit while you prepare the first pie filling.

CHOOSE ONE FLAVOR TO START WITH

Apple: In a large bowl, combine the apples, sugar, flour, cinnamon, vanilla and nutmeg. Stir them together until the apples are completely coated.

Cherry: In a medium bowl, stir together the cherry pie filling and almond extract with a spoon.

Once the filling is ready, sprinkle a spoonful of flour on your work surface. Use a rolling pin to gently roll out one piecrust dough from the first box to ⅛-inch (3-mm) thickness. Use a 4-inch (10-cm) round cookie cutter to cut out as many circles as you can from the dough. To get all 12 circles from the dough, you will need to knead (squeeze and pinch) the scraps back into a dough ball and reroll it to fit more circle cutouts. Keep rolling out the dough scraps until you have all 12 circles for your pan.

Place each circle of dough into a well of the muffin tin. Gently press the dough into the bottom of the well and then smooth the dough around the sides. The dough should fit snugly around the entire well with no air pockets. Prick the bottom of the dough with a fork two or three times; this will help prevent a big dough bubble from forming when they bake.

TO ASSEMBLE

Spoon the pie filling evenly among the prepared muffin wells. You will use the entire batch of apples evenly divided among the wells. For the cherry pies, use just 1 to 2 tablespoons (15 to 30 g) of the cherry filling so that the juices don't overflow from the baked pie.

Roll out the second piecrust from your first box and this time use a 3-inch (7.5-cm) cookie cutter to make the top piecrusts for each well. Cover each mini pie. Pinch the edges of the crusts together to seal. Then, use a small paring knife to cut four small slits to vent the pie.

Bake for 15 minutes, or until the top piecrust is light golden brown. Use oven mitts to remove the tin from the oven and let the pies cool in their muffin tin for 15 minutes. Use a small spatula or fork to carefully remove the pies from the pan and place them on a wire rack to finish cooling before serving.

Repeat the process with the second box of piecrusts to bake the second flavor of mini-pies.

LUCK O' THE IRISH CHOCOLATE CUPCAKES

**YIELD:
12 CUPCAKES**

Feeling lucky, friends? Everyone will have leprechaun blessings this St. Paddy's Day with these delightful rainbow-themed chocolate cupcakes. Find your gold at the end of the rainbow.

1 cup (125 g) all-purpose flour

½ tsp baking soda

¼ tsp salt

⅓ cup (37 g) unsweetened cocoa powder

⅓ cup (58 g) semisweet chocolate chips

½ cup (118 ml) water

¾ cup (150 g) sugar

½ cup (115 g) sour cream

½ cup (118 ml) vegetable oil

1 tsp vanilla extract

2 large eggs

DECORATIONS

1 batch Chocolate Fudge Frosting (page 41)

Rainbow sprinkles

12 or more golden foil chocolate coins

Preheat the oven to 325°F (170°C, or gas mark 3). Line each well of a 12-muffin tin with a double layer of cupcake wrappers and set aside.

In a medium bowl, combine the flour, baking soda and salt. Whisk them together.

In your large mixing bowl, combine the cocoa powder and chocolate chips.

Measure the water into a glass measuring cup. Microwave on HIGH for 2 minutes, or until the water reaches a boil. Use oven mitts to remove the cup and add the water to the chocolate chips. Use a spatula to stir the hot water into the chocolate mixture until it has completely melted and the mixture is smooth.

Add the sugar, sour cream, oil and vanilla to the chocolate mixture. Stir them into the chocolate mixture until smooth.

Crack the eggs into a small bowl to check for shells. Add the eggs to the chocolate mixture. Beat everything together with a mixer on medium speed until just combined.

Add the flour mixture to the chocolate mixture and beat with an electric mixer on medium speed until just combined.

Spoon the batter evenly among the prepared muffin wells so they are two-thirds full. Bake for 9 minutes and then use oven mitts to rotate the pan. Bake for an additional 9 to 12 minutes, or until a toothpick inserted into the center of a cupcake comes out clean.

Remove from the oven and let the cupcakes cool right in the muffin tin for 15 minutes. Carefully transfer them to a wire rack to cool completely before frosting.

To decorate, pipe the frosting in a swirly pattern on the cupcakes. Sprinkle with the rainbow sprinkles while the frosting is still fresh and then top with a few golden foil chocolate coins.

EARTH DAY DIRT CUPS

**YIELD:
8 TO 10 SERVINGS**

Watching the first green buds sprout out of the muddy ground is such an exciting part of spring. Bring that thrilling moment to your table with these pretty sprouting cups of chocolate "earth." You'll love the mint-chocolate pudding base with crumbly cookie topping. For an extra fun surprise, add a few gummy worms in the "dirt."

1 cup (200 g) sugar

½ cup (55 g) unsweetened cocoa powder

¼ cup (30 g) cornstarch

½ tsp salt

4 cups (946 ml) milk

2 tbsp (28 g) salted butter

2 tsp (10 ml) vanilla extract

½ tsp peppermint extract

1 cup (175 g) chocolate chips

DECORATIONS

1 (9-oz [255-g]) package chocolate wafer cookies

Several fresh mint sprigs

Assorted gummy worms (optional)

Set out the serving cups you plan to use.

In a large saucepan, combine the sugar, cocoa, cornstarch and salt and whisk them together. Add the milk and gently whisk it in. Place the saucepan over medium-high heat and continue to stir and whisk until the mixture begins to boil, about 5 minutes.

Remove the pan from the heat and add the butter and extracts. Stir them until the butter melts. Add the chocolate chips and stir them in. They will partially melt. Spoon the warm pudding into the individual serving cups and then refrigerate until set, 2 to 3 hours.

To decorate, crumble the chocolate wafer cookies in a large resealable plastic bag by breaking them up with a rolling pin or kitchen mallet. Sprinkle the crumbs over the top of each pudding cup. Rinse the fresh mint with cold water and very gently pat it dry with a clean towel. Then, pinch a sprig of fresh mint and plant it in the cookie "dirt." Add a few gummy worms poking out of the dirt, if you like.

BIRD'S NEST HAYSTACK COOKIES

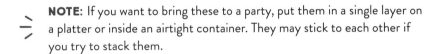

**YIELD:
12 COOKIES**

These sweet little bird's nests signal the start of spring. The no-bake cookie base looks fancy, but is actually so easy to make. They'll look absolutely adorable on your holiday buffet.

¾ cup (131 g) butterscotch chips

½ cup (130 g) smooth peanut butter or your favorite nut or seed butter

2 (5-oz [140-g]) containers chow mein noodles

½ cup (65 g) mini chocolate eggs

Cut twelve 5-inch (12.5-cm) squares of parchment paper. Gently press a square into each well of a 12-muffin tin and set aside.

In a large, microwave-safe bowl, combine the butterscotch chips and peanut butter. Heat on HIGH for 30 seconds. Use oven mitts to remove the bowl and stir. Continue to heat in 10- to 15-second sessions, stirring each time, until the mixture is smooth and melted.

Stir in the chow mein noodles and continue to toss and stir until they are completely covered with the peanut butter sauce. Use a large spoon to scoop and divide the noodles evenly into the wells of the muffin tin. Add 2 or 3 chocolate eggs to each bird's nest while the peanut butter is still soft.

Let the nests cool for 20 minutes and then remove by pulling up on the edges of the parchment paper.

NOTE: If you want to bring these to a party, put them in a single layer on a platter or inside an airtight container. They may stick to each other if you try to stack them.

DAINTY DAISY CUPCAKES

**YIELD:
12 CUPCAKES**

Set a blooming batch of these darling daisies on your table for a cheery treat. Fluffy marshmallows and chocolate candies are a sweet way to decorate these bright lemon-flavored cupcakes.

Make sure to decorate the cupcakes on the same day you plan to serve them. The marshmallows tend to dry out if cut more than a few hours ahead of time.

1 lemon

8 tbsp (1 stick [112 g]) salted butter, softened

1 cup (200 g) sugar

2 large eggs

½ tsp vanilla extract

½ cup (118 ml) milk

1½ cups (135 g) cake flour (check the substitutions on page 183 if you don't have it!)

¼ tsp salt

1 batch Sweet Buttercream Frosting (page 38) or Cream Cheese Frosting (page 42)

DECORATIONS

Marshmallows (regular size, not mini)

Pastel chocolate candies

Preheat the oven to 375°F (190°C, or gas mark 5). Line each well of a 12-muffin tin with a double layer of cupcake wrappers and set aside.

Wash and dry the lemon. Use a Microplane zester to rub the lemon and remove the yellow zest. Zesters can be very sharp, so you might want to ask an adult for help. Cut the lemon in half and squeeze the juice into a bowl. Remove any of the lemon seeds that may have fallen in.

In your large mixing bowl, combine the butter and sugar and beat them together until light and fluffy. In a small bowl, crack the eggs and check for shells. Add them to the butter and beat with an electric mixer on medium speed until just combined. Stop the mixer and scrape the bowl. Add the vanilla and 1 tablespoon (6 g) of the lemon zest and beat until just combined. Add the milk and 2 tablespoons (30 ml) of the lemon juice to the butter and beat to combine. Scrape the bowl.

Add the flour and salt to the batter and beat on medium-low speed to combine. Scrape the bowl to check for pockets of dry flour.

Spoon the batter evenly into the prepared muffin wells, about two-thirds full. Bake for 17 minutes, or until a toothpick inserted into the center of a cupcake comes out clean. Remove from the oven and let the cupcakes cool in the muffin tin for 15 minutes. Carefully transfer them to a wire rack to cool completely before frosting.

Spread or pipe the frosting evenly over each cooled cupcake.

To decorate, use clean kitchen scissors to cut each marshmallow in half on an angle to form flower petals. Place five petals in a flower formation on the top of each cupcake. Place a pretty chocolate candy in the center. You might want to use a little dot of frosting to hold the candy in place.

SPRING GREEN PISTACHIO TORTE

YIELD: 12 SERVINGS

Baking brings back special memories. My mom made this dessert for me when I was a kid and now my girls love it just as much as I did. When Grandma offered to make anything they wanted one weekend, this was at the top of their list. What a delightful surprise it is to make her famous dessert for her. Your family will surely be eager to have a big slice, don't expect to have any leftovers!

½ lb (2 sticks [225 g]) salted butter, cold

2 cups (250 g) all-purpose flour

½ cup (55 g) chopped pecans

8 oz (225 g) cream cheese, softened

1½ cups (180 g) powdered sugar

1 (8-oz [226-g]) container frozen whipped topping, thawed, divided

2 (3.3-oz [94-g]) boxes pistachio-flavored pudding mix

2 cups (473 ml) milk

Preheat the oven to 350°F (175°C, or gas mark 4).

Cut the butter into small cubes with a butter knife and place them in a medium bowl. Add the flour and use two forks to mush the flour into the butter. You can also pinch the butter and flour together, using your clean hands. Continue to press and blend until the dough looks like coarse crumbs and all the flour is moistened by the butter. Stir in the chopped pecans.

Pour the crumbs into a 9 x 13-inch (23 x 33–cm) baking pan and use your fingers to press them into a smooth crust evenly along the bottom. You can also use the bottom of a drinking glass to press it into place. Bake for 18 to 20 minutes, or until the crust is lightly toasted in color. Remove from the oven and let it cool completely to room temperature.

Place the cream cheese in your large mixing bowl. Beat it with a mixer on medium speed until smooth. Stop the mixer and scrape the bowl. Add the sugar and beat until well combined. Scrape the bowl again.

Add 1 cup (75 g) of the whipped topping and gently fold it into the cream cheese. Carefully spread the cream cheese mixture over the prepared crust. Smooth it out with your spatula.

In a medium bowl, combine the pudding mix and milk. Beat them together for 2 minutes on high speed. Use a spatula to spread the pudding mixture evenly over the cream cheese layer.

Top the torte with the remaining whipped topping. Spread it out evenly and then chill the torte in the fridge for 1 hour before serving.

SWEET

CARROT CAKE DONUTS WITH CREAM CHEESE GLAZE

YIELD: 18 DONUTS

Get ready for the Easter Bunny's visit with these delicious carrot cake donuts. Such a fun twist on the classic Easter breakfast, they'll have you ready for the egg hunt in a twitch.

Baking spray, for pans
2 cups (250 g) all-purpose flour
⅔ cup (75 g) light brown sugar
2 tsp (9 g) baking powder
¼ tsp salt
1½ tsp (4 g) ground cinnamon
½ tsp ground nutmeg
¼ tsp ground allspice
2 large eggs
1 cup (237 ml) milk
1 tsp vanilla extract

4 tbsp (½ stick [55 g]) salted butter, melted
1 cup (110 g) shredded carrot

GLAZE
4 oz (115 g) ⅓-fat cream cheese
1 tbsp (14 g) salted butter, softened
½ cup (60 g) powdered sugar
½ tsp vanilla extract
⅛ tsp salt

Sprinkles (optional)

Preheat the oven to 350°F (175°C, or gas mark 4). Spray the wells of two donut pans with baking spray and set aside.

In your large mixing bowl, combine the flour, brown sugar, baking powder, salt, cinnamon, nutmeg and allspice and whisk them together.

Crack the eggs into a small bowl and check for shells. Add the milk and vanilla to the eggs and whisk together. Slowly pour the milk mixture into the flour mixture and stir until just combined.

Put the butter in a microwave-safe bowl and heat on HIGH for 30 seconds to melt. Use oven mitts to remove the bowl and with a fork whisk in any bits of butter that haven't melted completely. Slowly pour the butter in while whisking the batter.

Fold in the shredded carrot, using a spatula. Spoon the batter into a measuring cup with a spout and pour the batter into the prepared donut wells. Fill them about two-thirds full. Use a spoon or toothpick to even out the batter within the wells.

Bake for 8 to 10 minutes. Remove from the oven and let the donuts cool in the pan for 5 minutes before transferring to a wire rack.

While the donuts are baking and cooling, prepare the glaze. In a medium bowl, combine the cream cheese and butter and beat them with an electric mixer on medium speed until smooth. Add the powdered sugar, vanilla and salt and beat together until smooth.

Spread the glaze on the donuts with a butter knife and decorate with sprinkles, if using.

TROPICAL LIME COOKIES

YIELD: 30 COOKIES

When spring break falls during chilly wintery-feeling days, transport yourself to a sunny tropical island with these lime cookies. Turn on your favorite vacation tunes, set out a beach towel and have an impromptu cookie picnic!

2 limes

8 tbsp (1 stick [112 g]) salted butter, softened

½ cup (118 ml) vegetable oil

1 cup (200 g) sugar

1 tbsp (15 ml) vanilla extract

1 tsp baking powder

1 tsp baking soda

½ tsp salt

1 large egg

3 cups (375 g) all-purpose flour

1 cup (175 g) white chocolate chips

¼ cup (34 g) finely chopped macadamia nuts (optional)

GLAZE

1 cup (120 g) powdered sugar

1 tbsp (15 ml) milk

1 tbsp (15 ml) fresh lime juice

Preheat the oven to 375°F (190°C, or gas mark 5). Set out two cookie pans and line with parchment paper; set aside.

Wash and dry the limes. Use a Microplane zester to rub the lime and remove the green zest. Zesters can be very sharp, so you might want to ask an adult for help. Cut the limes in half, squeeze the juice into a bowl and set aside. You will use most of it in the cookie dough, but save 1 tablespoon (15 ml) for the glaze.

In your large mixing bowl, combine the butter, oil, sugar, vanilla, lime zest, 3 tablespoons (45 ml) of the fresh lime juice, the baking powder, baking soda and salt. Crack the egg into a small bowl and check for shells. Add the egg to the large bowl.

Mix all the ingredients together by beating with an electric mixer on medium speed until well combined. Stop the mixer and scrape the sides of the bowl. Add the flour and beat on medium speed until just combined. Scrape the bowl to check for any dry pockets of flour. Add the chocolate chips and chopped nuts and stir with a spoon to mix them into the dough.

Use a teaspoon to scoop rounded spoonfuls of dough and drop them on the prepared cookie pans. Space the cookies 2 inches (5 cm) apart. Lightly flatten the dough with the bottom of a drinking glass.

Bake for 12 to 15 minutes, or until the edges of the cookies are lightly golden brown. Remove from the oven and let cool on the pans for 2 minutes. Then, carefully transfer the cookies to a wire rack to cool completely.

To frost the cookies, in a medium bowl, combine the powdered sugar, milk and the 1 tablespoon (15 ml) of reserved lime juice and mix them together with a fork until smooth. Place the wire rack with the cookies over a large piece of parchment paper. Dip your fork into the glaze and drizzle it over the cookies. Let them completely dry before storing.

Mom

HUMMING-BIRD CUPCAKES

YIELD: 24 CUPCAKES

Want to make a special cake for Mother's Day? We served my daughter hummingbird cake for her very first birthday; it's just the kind of sweet memory moms love to remember. What kind of cake did your mom serve you? These classic tropical-flavored cakes have a tasty pineapple and banana combo. Be sure to top them with tangy cream cheese frosting and a few salty pecans if you really want to spoil your mom.

3 cups (375 g) flour

2 cups (400 g) sugar

1 tsp salt

1 tsp baking soda

1 tsp ground cinnamon

3 large eggs

1½ cups (355 ml) vegetable oil

1½ tsp (8 ml) vanilla extract

1 (8-oz [225-g]) can crushed pineapple in juice

3 very ripe bananas with brown spots

1 cup (110 g) chopped pecans

DECORATION

2 batches Cream Cheese Frosting (page 42)

24 salted pecan halves, or 1 cup (110 g) chopped pecans (optional)

Preheat the oven to 350°F (175°C, or gas mark 4). Line each well of two 12-muffin tins with a double layer of cupcake wrappers and set aside.

In your large mixing bowl, combine the flour, sugar, salt, baking soda and cinnamon. Whisk them together.

Crack the eggs into a small bowl and check for shells. Add the eggs and oil to the flour and stir until all the flour has become wet. Scrape the bowl.

Add the vanilla, the crushed pineapple and its juice and the peeled bananas to the flour mixture. Beat with an electric mixer on medium speed until just combined. Stop the mixer and scrape the bowl and the beaters. Fold in the chopped pecans with a spoon.

Spoon the batter evenly into the prepared muffin wells, filling each well about three-quarters full. Bake for 18 to 20 minutes, or until a toothpick inserted in the center of a cupcake comes out clean. Remove from the oven and let the cupcakes cool completely on a wire rack before you frost them.

To decorate, pipe the cream cheese frosting in a swirl pattern over the top of each cupcake. Add a pecan half at the top point or sprinkle chopped pecans over the top.

DROP BISCUITS WITH CINNAMON-HONEY BUTTER

**YIELD:
8 BISCUITS**

Grandmas and baking biscuits go together like summer and lemonade stands. For Mother's Day this year, make a basket of biscuits with sweet honey butter and maybe a jar of the Sweet and Smooth Strawberry Jam Sauce (page 44) as a special gift. If your grandma lives far away, send her a copy of the recipe and bake it together long distance! You can have a virtual tea party over the phone that would make her day.

2 cups (250 g) all-purpose flour

1 tbsp (14 g) baking powder

1 tsp salt

1 tsp sugar

10 tbsp (1 stick plus 2 tbsp [140 g]) salted butter, cold, cut into cubes

¾ cup (177 ml) whole milk

HONEY BUTTER

½ lb (2 sticks [225 g]) salted butter, softened

3 tbsp (63 g) honey

1 tsp ground cinnamon

Preheat the oven to 400°F (200°C, or gas mark 6). Set out a cookie pan with parchment paper; set aside.

In your large mixing bowl, combine the flour, baking powder, salt and sugar and whisk them together. Add the butter and use two forks to press the butter into the flour. You might find it easier to try pinching it together with clean fingers. Continue to press and mix until the flour starts to stick together and form pea-size pieces.

Pour the milk into the flour mixture and use your fork to stir it together until everything has become evenly wet. Scoop the dough into eight mounds, about ⅓ cup (43 g) each. Place them 2 to 3 inches (5 to 7.5 cm) apart on the prepared cookie pan.

Bake for 20 minutes, or until the biscuits are golden brown and a toothpick inserted in the center of a biscuit comes out with a few wet crumbs attached.

For the honey butter, place the butter in your large mixing bowl and beat it with an electric mixer on medium speed until light and fluffy. Stop the mixer and scrape the sides of the bowl with a spatula and add the honey and cinnamon. Beat again until everything is combined. Store in an airtight container in the fridge for 2 weeks. Bring to room temperature before serving with the biscuits.

SUMMER
CELEBRATIONS

What's not to love about summer? No school, more time with your friends and family, vacations, pool days and lazy afternoons around the house. You'll have oodles of time to practice your baking skills this season.

Honor the red, white and blue with patriotic treats for Memorial Day and the Fourth of July. Celebrate dad this Father's Day with salty sweet candy (page 109) and cookies that include his favorite snacks (page 110). Cool off with a homemade icebox dessert (page 102) or ice cream cake (page 121) for National Ice Cream Day.

All the recipes you need to make your summer sparkle start here.

STRAWBERRY ICEBOX DESSERT

YIELD: 12 SERVINGS

This refreshing and chilly dessert is perfect for hot summer nights. Kick off the first weekend of summer vacation or the last day of school with this bright and fruity cheesecake-flavored torte. You can make it the night before, so it's ready to party when you are. The graham crackers soften up overnight and make the torte taste like cake!

2 cups (330 g) fresh sliced strawberries

2 cups (330 g) canned or fresh pineapple chunks

1 cup (190 g) canned mandarin oranges

2 (3.4-oz [96-g]) packages cheesecake pudding

3 cups (710 ml) cold milk

2 (8-oz [225-g]) containers frozen whipped topping, divided

1 (14.4-oz [408-g]) box graham crackers

Wash and dry the fruit you plan to use. Stir the assorted fruits together in a medium bowl and set aside.

In your large mixing bowl, combine the pudding mix and milk and either whisk together by hand or beat with an electric mixer on medium-high speed for 2 minutes. Stop the mixer and scrape down the sides of the bowl and let stand for 5 minutes. Add 1 whole container of the whipped topping to the bowl and gently fold it into the pudding mixture. Save the remaining container of whipped topping for decorating the top of the final dish.

Spread a single layer of graham crackers, 6 to 8 crackers, across the bottom of a 9 x 13–inch (23 x 33–cm) baking dish. Then, carefully spoon several dollops of the pudding mixture over the crackers and gently spread it into a thin even layer. Place another layer of graham crackers in a single layer across the pudding mixture.

Spread half of the remaining pudding mixture carefully over the top of the graham crackers. Add HALF of the fruit mixture evenly over the pudding. Gently press the fruit into the pudding mixture.

Add another layer of graham crackers and then top them with the remaining pudding mixture. Add another layer of mixed fruit, saving some for decorating the top, and press it into the pudding mixture. Add one last layer of graham crackers. Use the reserved container of whipped topping to frost the top of the dessert.

Chill for 4 hours or overnight in the fridge. Decorate with the reserved fruit just before serving.

HOT FUDGE SUNDAE CUPCAKES

**YIELD:
12 CUPCAKES**

Love ice cream but your mom doesn't want it melting all over your party table? These sneaky hot fudge sundae cupcakes will surprise your friends and keep them giggling for days.

1¾ cups (219 g) all-purpose flour

1 cup (200 g) sugar

1½ tsp (7 g) baking powder

¾ tsp salt

12 tbsp (1½ sticks [167 g]) salted butter, softened

3 large eggs

¾ cup (177 ml) milk

1½ tsp (8 ml) vanilla extract

1 to 2 large waffle ice-cream cones

1 batch Sweet Buttercream Frosting (page 38)

DECORATIONS

1 (12.8-oz [362-g]) jar thick hot fudge sauce (not chocolate sauce)

1 (12-oz [340-g]) jar maraschino cherries

Broken pieces of waffle cone

Sprinkles

Preheat the oven to 350°F (175°C, or gas mark 4). Line each well of a muffin tin with a double layer of cupcake wrappers and set aside.

In your large mixing bowl, combine the flour, sugar, baking powder and salt. Whisk them together. Cut the butter into 12 pieces and add it to the flour mixture. Beat the flour mixture and butter together with an electric mixer on medium speed until the mixture resembles coarse sand, about 1 minute.

Crack the eggs into a small bowl and check for shells. Add the eggs to the flour mixture and mix on medium speed until just combined. Add the milk and vanilla and beat on medium speed until the batter is light and fluffy with no lumps, about 3 minutes.

Spoon the batter evenly among the prepared muffin wells, about two-thirds full. Bake for 10 minutes and then use oven mitts to rotate the pan. Bake for an additional 8 to 10 minutes, or until the tops are lightly golden and a toothpick inserted into the center of a cupcake comes out clean.

Remove from the oven and let the cupcakes cool right in the muffin tin for 15 minutes. Carefully transfer to a wire rack to cool completely before frosting.

To decorate, place the waffle cones in a resealable plastic bag and crush them with a rolling pin or kitchen mallet until they are fine crumbs. Stir them into the buttercream frosting.

Pipe the frosting with a large open circle tip (we used Wilton tip size 2A). Or you can use an ice cream scoop to scoop dollops of frosting on top. Heat the hot fudge in a microwave-safe bowl on HIGH for 30 seconds to loosen it up. Let it cool for 1 minute, then use a spoon to drizzle the fudge over the frosting. Top with a maraschino cherry and dot with additional pieces of broken waffle cone and sprinkles.

MALTED CHOCOLATE CHIP COOKIES

**YIELD:
4 DOZEN COOKIES**

Our family loves to check out old-fashioned candy shops and ice-cream spots when we travel for summer vacations. These cookies are inspired by the malt balls and malted milk shakes served at those classic sweet spots. Even better, they make a perfect car trip treat. Pack a bag in the cooler when you hit the road! These are much thinner than traditional chocolate chip cookies and have a wonderful chewy, crispy texture.

½ lb (2 sticks [225 g]) salted butter, softened

¾ cup (177 g) packed light brown sugar

¾ cup (150 g) granulated sugar

2 large eggs

2 tsp (10 ml) vanilla extract

½ cup (48 g) malted milk powder

2 cups (250 g) all-purpose flour

1¼ tsp (6 g) baking soda

1¼ tsp (8 g) salt

1 (12-oz [340-g]) bag milk chocolate chips

Preheat the oven to 375°F (190°C, or gas mark 5). Set out two cookie pans and line them with parchment paper; set aside.

In your large mixing bowl, combine the butter, brown sugar and granulated sugar. Beat with an electric mixer on medium-high speed until light and fluffy. Crack the eggs into a small bowl and check for shells. Add the eggs and vanilla to the butter mixture and beat on medium speed until just combined.

In a medium bowl, combine the malted milk powder, flour, baking soda and salt and whisk them together. Add the flour mixture to the butter mixture and mix on medium speed until just combined. Fold in the chocolate chips by hand, using a spatula.

Use a teaspoon to measure and drop balls of cookie dough 3 inches (7.5 cm) apart on your prepared cookie pans. The cookies will seem tiny but they really spread out thinly. Bake for 6 to 8 minutes. Remove from the oven and let the cookies cool for 5 minutes on the cookie pans before transferring to a wire rack to cool completely.

NOTE: You can find malted milk powder either in the baking aisle or ice-cream toppings section of your grocery store.

SWEET & SALTY

FATHER'S DAY PRETZEL BARK

YIELD: 24 SERVINGS

Want to make dad's day extra special? Bake up a batch of this salty-sweet toffee bark with crunchy pretzels. It's the perfect sweet treat for him to munch while watching his favorite show.

8 oz (225 g) mini pretzels
½ lb (2 sticks [225 g]) salted butter
1 cup (225 g) packed light brown sugar
2 cups (350 g) semisweet chocolate chips
Pinch of kosher salt

Preheat the oven to 375°F (190°C, or gas mark 5). Set out a jelly-roll pan and line it with parchment paper. Get a kitchen timer ready for when you cook the toffee on the stovetop.

Break up the pretzels into small pieces and spread them out on the prepared pan. The bottom of the pan should be covered with a single layer of pretzels.

Place the butter in a medium saucepan, and melt it over medium-high heat. Add the brown sugar to the butter and whisk together. Let the butter and sugar cook together until the mixture starts to simmer and bubble. As soon as you see bubbles all over the surface of the mixture, set a timer for 3 minutes. Let it cook for the 3 minutes without stirring and then, while wearing oven mitts to protect your hands, immediately pour it all over the layer of pretzels in the jelly-roll pan. The sugar mixture will be VERY HOT, so you might want to ask for an adult to help.

The pretzels will probably move around when you pour the butter and sugar over them. Use a spoon to smooth them out into a single layer again.

Carefully place the pan in the oven and bake the pretzels for 5 minutes. When the time is up, carefully remove the pan from the oven. While it is still hot, sprinkle the chocolate chips evenly over the top of the baked pretzels. Let the chocolate begin to melt for 2 to 3 minutes and then use a spatula to evenly spread it over the top of the pretzels. Sprinkle a pinch of kosher salt over the top.

Let the pretzel bark cool completely at room temperature. When it is completely cooled, break it into large pieces and store in an airtight container.

NOTE: It is really important to use kosher salt instead of regular table salt in this recipe. Kosher salt is a larger flake salt with a milder taste than the kind of salt used at your dinner table. It is easier to pinch and sprinkle and a great choice for your baking.

ALL-AMERICAN POTATO CHIP COOKIES

YIELD: 24 COOKIES

Need a treat for a picnic on the go? Whether you're heading to a family barbecue or an adventurous day trip, these potato chip cookies travel well and are a fun twist on classic chocolate chip cookies. You won't be able to resist these salty and sweet, crispy but chewy cookies. Bonus points: They won't melt in the summer heat.

8 tbsp (1 stick [112 g]) salted butter, softened

½ cup (100 g) granulated sugar

½ cup (115 g) packed light brown sugar

½ tsp salt

1 tsp baking powder

1 tsp vanilla extract

1 large egg

1 cup (80 g) old-fashioned rolled oats

1 cup (125 g) all-purpose flour

1 cup (175 g) semisweet chocolate chips

2 cups (84 g) gently crushed potato chips

Preheat the oven to 350°F (175°C, or gas mark 4). Set out two cookie pans and line them with parchment paper; set aside.

In your large mixing bowl, combine the butter, granulated sugar and brown sugar and beat with an electric mixer on medium speed until light and fluffy. Stop the mixer and scrape the sides of the bowl. Add the salt, baking powder and vanilla and beat until just combined.

Crack the egg into a small bowl and check for shells. Add the egg to the butter mixture and beat it in until just combined. Add the oats and flour and beat until just combined. The dough will be very stiff. Stir in the chocolate chips by hand, using a spatula, and then finally the potato chips, being careful not to break the potato chip pieces too much more.

Use a tablespoon to scoop the dough and then form the cookies with clean hands. The dough will be very crumbly with the chips, so pat and form the cookies with your fingers and place them on the prepared cookie pans. Leave 2 to 3 inches (5 to 7.5 cm) between the cookies because they will spread.

Bake for 12 to 14 minutes, or until the cookies are browned around the edges. Remove from the oven and let the cookies cool on the cookie pans; they will be very soft and fragile until they have cooled and set.

FLUFFER-NUTTER MUDDY BUDDIES

**YIELD:
16 SERVINGS**

We love to bring homemade treats on our family vacation road trips for enjoying at our hotel. This portable snack mix is just perfect for taking to the beach house, camping or wherever your family is headed this summer!

8 cups (216 g) Rice Chex cereal, or similar product

4 tbsp (½ stick [55 g]) salted butter

1 cup (260 g) creamy peanut butter, or your favorite nut or seed butter

1 (7-oz [198-g]) jar marshmallow fluff

½ cup (88 g) white chocolate chips

1⅓ cups (160 g) powdered sugar

Place the cereal in a large mixing bowl and set aside.

In a medium microwave-safe bowl, combine the butter, peanut butter, marshmallow fluff and white chocolate chips. Heat on HIGH for 30 seconds. Then, use oven mitts to remove the bowl and stir. Continue to heat the mixture in 15-second sessions stirring each time, until it is melted and smooth.

Carefully pour the melted marshmallow mixture over the cereal and stir until everything is evenly coated. Pour the cereal into a large resealable plastic bag and add 1 cup (120 g) of the powdered sugar. Seal the bag and then gently shake and toss until the cereal is completely coated with sugar. Add the remaining ⅓ cup (40 g) of powdered sugar and toss again.

Spread out the muddy buddies on a large sheet of waxed or parchment paper and let it cool. Store it in an airtight container.

SUNSHINE BARS

YIELD:
9 SERVINGS

Have you noticed how much more sunshine we get in the summer? The longest day of the year falls between June 20–22, when we get the most hours of sunshine. Celebrate the day with these bright and shiny lemon bars; they taste great chilled in the fridge!

8 tbsp (1 stick [112 g]) salted butter, softened, plus 1 tbsp (14 g) for the pan

½ cup (100 g) granulated sugar

1 cup (125 g) all-purpose flour

Pinch of salt

FILLING

2 large or 3 small lemons

2 large eggs

¾ cup (150 g) granulated sugar

3 tbsp (24 g) all-purpose flour

Powdered sugar, for decorating

Preheat the oven to 350°F (175°C, or gas mark 4). Line a 9-inch (23-cm) square baking pan with parchment paper. Rub the parchment paper with a bit of softened butter and set aside.

In your large mixing bowl, combine the butter and granulated sugar and beat with an electric mixer until light and fluffy. Scrape the bowl as needed. Add the flour and a pinch of salt and beat into the butter on low speed until the dough comes together into a solid piece.

Transfer the dough to the prepared baking pan and use your clean hands to press the crust evenly into the corners and sides and into a nice even layer. Bake for 15 to 20 minutes, or until the crust turns light golden brown.

While the crust is baking, prepare your filling. Wash and dry the lemons. Use a Microplane zester to rub one of the lemons and collect the yellow lemon zest. Measure out 1 teaspoon of the zest and set it aside.

Cut both of the lemons in half. Use a fork to prick the inside of the lemon and squeeze the juice into a bowl. Remove any lemon seeds you find in the juice, using a spoon. Measure ¼ cup (59 ml) of lemon juice and set it aside.

Crack the eggs into a medium bowl and check for shells. Add the granulated sugar and whisk it together with the eggs until it is well combined and the mixture is thick. Add the flour, reserved lemon zest and the lemon juice and whisk them together until blended.

Pour the filling over the baked crust. Spread it out evenly with a spoon so it covers the entire top of the crust. Return the pan to the oven and bake for 18 to 20 minutes, or until the lemon custard is set and doesn't jiggle in the center when you wiggle the pan.

Remove from the oven and let the bars cool completely in the pan. Carefully pull the bars up out of the pan by holding the parchment paper edges. Cut them into squares with a butter knife and sprinkle powdered sugar over the top just before serving.

PANCAKE DONUTS WITH MAPLE GLAZE

YIELD: 12 DONUTS

One of our favorite family traditions is to host a "reading picnic" on the weekends. We spread out a picnic blanket on the floor of our living room, grab a bunch of books and read out loud to one another while munching on our breakfast. These donuts let you enjoy the pancake fun outside of the kitchen and are just perfect for your own reading picnic.

Baking spray, for pans
1½ cups (188 g) all-purpose flour
1 tsp baking powder
1 tsp salt
2 tbsp (26 g) granulated sugar
1 large egg
1¼ cups (295 ml) milk
4 tbsp (½ stick [55 g]) salted butter

GLAZE
2 cups (240 g) powdered sugar
¼ cup (59 ml) maple syrup
1 to 2 tbsp (15 to 30 ml) milk

Crumbled cooked bacon (optional)

Preheat the oven to 350°F (175°C, or gas mark 4). Spray the wells of two donut pans with baking spray and set aside.

In your large mixing bowl, combine the flour, baking powder, salt and granulated sugar and whisk them together.

Crack the egg into a small bowl and check for shells. Add the milk and whisk together. Pour the milk mixture into the flour mixture and stir them together. The batter will be slightly lumpy.

Place the butter in a microwave-safe bowl. Heat on HIGH for 30 seconds. Use a fork to whisk in any bits of butter that haven't melted. Slowly pour it into the donut batter while whisking to prevent the egg from cooking from the heat of the butter.

Spoon the batter into a liquid measuring cup and pour the batter into the prepared donut wells. Fill them two-thirds full; the donuts will expand while cooking. Bake for 10 to 15 minutes, or until the donuts bounce back when gently pressed. Remove from the oven and let them cool in their pans for 5 minutes before transferring to a wire rack.

While the donuts are baking and cooling, prepare the glaze. In a medium bowl, combine the powdered sugar, maple syrup and 1 tablespoon (15 ml) of milk. Whisk together until smooth. If the glaze is too runny, add more powdered sugar, a few tablespoons at a time, until it is slightly thickened. If the glaze is too thick, add the second tablespoon (15 ml) of milk.

Place a large sheet of waxed or parchment paper on the counter and place the wire rack of donuts over it. Working one donut at a time, dip the donut into the glaze and place it on the rack, glaze side up. If you'd like you can now sprinkle the crumbled bacon over the top and let dry. Repeat with the remaining donuts.

S'MORES BARS

**YIELD:
9 BARS**

When you want to enjoy everyone's favorite campfire treat but there's no fire pit in sight, these S'mores Bars bring the taste of a camping trip home. The deliciously ooey-gooey bars make a wonderful party treat all year long.

6 whole graham crackers

8 tbsp (1 stick [112 g]) salted butter, softened

½ cup (115 g) light brown sugar

¼ cup (50 g) granulated sugar

1 large egg

1 tsp vanilla extract

1¼ cups (156 g) all-purpose flour

1 tsp baking powder

1 tsp salt

3 (4.4-oz [125-g]) milk chocolate bars, such as Hershey's

1 (7-oz [198-g]) jar marshmallow fluff

Preheat the oven to 350°F (175°C, or gas mark 4). Set out an 8-inch (20.5-cm) square baking pan and line it with a piece of parchment paper that is large enough to come up the sides of the dish; set aside.

Place the graham crackers in a large resealable plastic bag and seal it closed. Use a rolling pin to crush the crackers into fine crumbs and set aside.

In your large mixing bowl, combine the butter, brown sugar and granulated sugar. Beat together with an electric mixer on medium speed until light and fluffy, about 1 minute. Stop the mixer and scrape the bowl. Crack the egg into a small bowl and check for shells. Add the egg and vanilla to the butter mixture and beat them in until just combined. Scrape the bowl. Add the graham cracker crumbs and mix for 20 seconds, or until just combined.

In a medium bowl, combine the flour, baking powder and salt and whisk them together. Add the flour mixture to the butter mixture and beat on low speed until just combined. Scrape the bowl.

Divide the dough in half and press one portion of it evenly into the bottom of the prepared pan. Pull the dough back out of the pan by tugging carefully on the parchment paper and set it on the counter for the top crust. Line the baking pan with another piece of parchment paper. Press the second half of the dough into the bottom to form the bottom crust.

Break the chocolate bars into squares and spread them evenly over the top of the bottom crust in your pan. Use a spoon to drop spoonfuls of marshmallow fluff on top and gently spread it evenly.

Take the reserved top crust dough and carefully flip it over on its parchment. Place the crust, dough side down, onto the marshmallow fluff. Gently peel back the parchment paper from the top of the crust. You can wiggle the crust into place with your fingers if it isn't perfectly centered on the top.

Bake for 30 minutes, or until the top crust is golden brown. Remove from the oven and let the S'mores Bars cool before removing them.

ooey-gooey

GRASS-HOPPER TORTE

YIELD: 12 SERVINGS

This minty chocolate ice-cream pie is a fun dessert to make ahead for your party. Serve it to your family for National Ice Cream Day, the third Sunday in July. We also love it during the Christmas season or for St. Patrick's Day.

Baking spray, for pan

1 (19-oz [541-g]) package chocolate sandwich cookies, such as Oreos

10 tbsp (1 stick plus 2 tbsp [140 g]) salted butter

½ gallon (1.9 L) mint ice cream

2 (12.8-oz [362-g]) jars hot fudge topping (not chocolate sauce)

Whipped cream, for serving (optional)

Spray a 9 x 13–inch (23 x 33 cm) baking pan with baking spray and set aside.

Place the cookies in a large resealable plastic bag and seal the bag closed. Break the cookies into crumbs with a kitchen mallet or rolling pin. Pour the crumbs into a medium bowl.

Place the butter in a microwave-safe measuring cup. Heat on HIGH for 30 to 40 seconds, or until melted. Pour the butter into the bowl of crushed cookies and use a spoon to stir and combine.

Pour the cookies into your prepared baking dish and use the bottom of a drinking glass or your clean hands to press the crumbs into a solid crust evenly along the bottom. Let the crust completely set in the fridge for 30 minutes. Meanwhile, let the ice cream sit on the counter to thaw while you wait for the crust to set.

When the ice cream is soft enough to spread, pour it over the prepared crust and use a spatula to spread it evenly over the top. Place the torte in the freezer for the ice cream to firm up.

Once the torte is frozen solid, place the jars of hot fudge topping in a microwave-safe bowl and heat on HIGH for 30 seconds. Remove the bowl and stir the hot fudge, using oven mitts to handle the hot jars. If it is still too thick, heat in 15-second sessions until it is smooth and spreadable. Test it with a quick stir. Pour the hot fudge over the top of the torte and use a spatula to spread it evenly over the surface.

Return the torte to the freezer to firm up for 1 hour before serving. Garnish with whipped cream, if you like.

RED, WHITE AND BLUEBERRY POKE CAKE

YIELD: 12 SERVINGS

This chilly cake is a blast to bake! Poke some holes in a baked sheet cake, pour in some liquid colored gelatin and let it mingle in the fridge. You'll have a perfectly refreshing dessert for hot summer parties. Mix and match the colors of gelatin for holidays all year round.

1 unfrosted 9 x 13–inch (23 x 33–cm) sheet cake (page 57), prepared without chocolate chips, or 1 (15.2-oz [432-g]) box vanilla cake mix

1 (3-oz [85-g]) package red gelatin mix, such as Jell-O

2 cups (473 ml) water, divided

2 cups (473 ml) cold water, divided

1 (3-oz [85-g]) package blue gelatin mix, such as Jell-O

1 batch Homemade Whipped Cream (page 28), or 1 (8-oz [226-g]) container frozen whipped topping

Sprinkles, for decoration (optional)

Prepare the sheet cake or bake the cake according to the package directions, using a 9 x 13–inch (23 x 33–cm) baking pan. Let the cake cool completely. Poke holes in the top of the cake every ½ inch (1.3 cm), using a large fork.

Pour the package of red gelatin mix into a medium, heatproof bowl. Place 1 cup (237 ml) of the water in a microwave-safe glass measuring cup and heat on HIGH for 3 to 4 minutes to bring it to a boil. Using oven mitts to cover your hands, pour it into the red gelatin mix and stir until the powder dissolves. Then pour 1 cup (237 ml) of the cold water into the gelatin mixture and stir.

Pour the package of blue gelatin mix into a second medium, heatproof bowl. Repeat the same steps as with the red gelatin mix: Add 1 cup (237 ml) of boiling water, stir. Add 1 cup (237 ml) of cold water, stir.

Using separate spoons, spoon the red and blue gelatin mixtures over the top of the cake, making sure to fill opposite rows of the holes with one or the other color to form a pattern in the cake. Chill in the fridge for 2 hours.

Use the whipped topping as a frosting and spread it evenly over the top of the cake with a butter knife just before you plan to serve. Decorate with sprinkles if you wish.

CELEBRATE

Fall FIESTA

The best part about the shift into fall is all the warm spiced flavors that appear in our favorite treats. The smell of a cozy Maple-Spiced Pumpkin Pie (page 135), juicy Apple Cider Donuts (page 129) and Scrumptious Snickerdoodles (page 144) baking in the oven make your home feel all warm and cozy.

Celebrating this season comes easy with Halloween and Thanksgiving kick-starting the end-of-the-year holiday celebrations. But don't forget to enjoy the smaller moments, too. Family game night, a trip to the pumpkin patch or a movie party with friends are all opportunities to spoil your loved ones with something homemade just for them.

From crispy oatmeal cookies for after-school snacks (page 139) to show-stopping Frosted Cranberry Bliss Bundtlettes (page 126) for your holiday table, all the fall desserts you need start here.

FROSTED CRANBERRY BLISS BUNDTLETTES

YIELD: 10 TO 12 BUNDTLETTES

Just what your Thanksgiving dessert buffet needs: these festive orange-cranberry white chocolate mini-cakes. You can make them with or without the cream cheese glaze, but if you have any trouble getting them out of the Bundtlette pan, the frosting will hide any mistakes and your family will never know!

CAKE

Baking spray, for pan

4 large eggs

¾ cup (177 ml) fresh orange juice (from 2 oranges, or just use store-bought juice from the fridge)

1 cup (100 g) fresh cranberries, rinsed and drained

2½ cups (313 g) all-purpose flour, plus 1 tbsp (8 g) for cranberries

2 cups (400 g) granulated sugar

1 tsp baking powder

1 tsp kosher salt

½ tsp baking soda

½ lb plus 4 tbsp (2½ sticks [280 g]) salted butter

1 cup (175 g) white chocolate chips

Preheat the oven to 350°F (175°C, or gas mark 4). Spray two 6-well Bundtlette pans with baking spray. Make sure to coat all the decorative nooks and crannies so that your cakes release well.

Crack the eggs into a small bowl to check for and remove shells. Add the orange juice and whisk together.

In a small bowl, stir the cranberries with 1 tablespoon (8 g) of the flour to coat them. This will help keep them from dropping to the bottom of the cakes.

In your large mixing bowl, combine the flour, sugar, baking powder, salt and baking soda and whisk together. Beating with an electric mixer on low speed, add the butter, 1 tablespoon (14 g) at a time, and continue to mix until the dough forms a pea-size crumble. Pour in the egg mixture and beat on medium speed until just combined. Scrape the bowl. Beat the batter on high speed until it is light and fluffy, about 2 more minutes. Scrape the beaters to get all the batter into the bowl.

Gently stir in the cranberries and white chocolate chips.

Spoon the batter into the Bundtlette wells until they are about two-thirds full. Use a small spoon to even out the tops. Bake for 20 to 25 minutes, or until a toothpick inserted into the deepest section of a Bundtlette comes out clean.

(continued)

FROSTED CRANBERRY BLISS BUNDTLETTES (CONTINUED)

GLAZE

4 oz (115 g) cream cheese, softened

1 cup (120 g) powdered sugar

4 tbsp (½ stick [55 g]) salted butter, softened

½ tsp vanilla extract

DECORATION

Fresh mint leaves (optional)

Sugared fresh cranberries (optional)

Remove from the oven and let the cakes cool in the pans for 15 to 20 minutes. To remove them, place a cookie pan over the Bundtlette pan. While wearing oven mitts, pinch the cookie pan and Bundtlette pan together and flip them upside down. Gently tap the Bundtlette pan and the cakes should fall right onto the cookie pan.

For the glaze, in a medium bowl, combine all the glaze ingredients. Beat them together with an electric mixer on medium-high speed until fluffy.

You can spread the glaze on the cakes with a butter knife, or put it in a pastry bag with an open star-shaped tip. We like Wilton size 32 but any star tip will do. Simply swirl the frosting over the top of the cakes in a zig-zag pattern to make pretty scallops.

Decorate with fresh mint leaves or homemade sugared cranberries.

APPLE CIDER DONUTS

My kids look forward to the hot and fresh apple cider donuts at our favorite apple orchard every fall. You don't need to wait for a trip to pick your own apples; these donuts are great throughout the season. They are baked right in your oven and they still have the classic cinnamon-sugar coating you'll love.

Baking spray, for pans

1 lemon

1½ cups (188 g) all-purpose flour

1½ tsp (7 g) baking powder

1 tsp salt

1 tsp ground cinnamon

¼ tsp ground nutmeg

⅓ cup (79 ml) apple cider

¼ cup (59 ml) buttermilk

1 tsp vanilla extract

8 tbsp (1 stick [112 g]) salted butter, softened

½ cup (115 g) packed brown sugar

½ cup (100 g) granulated sugar

2 eggs

TOPPING

4 tbsp (½ stick [55 g]) salted butter

½ cup (100 g) granulated sugar

½ tsp ground cinnamon

(continued)

APPLE CIDER DONUTS (CONTINUED)

Preheat the oven to 350°F (175°C, or gas mark 4). Spray two 6-well donut pans with baking spray and set aside.

Wash and dry the lemon. Use a Microplane zester to rub the lemon and remove the yellow zest. Zesters can be very sharp, so you might want to ask an adult for help. Place the zest in a small bowl.

In your large mixing bowl, combine the flour, baking powder, salt, cinnamon, nutmeg and the lemon zest. Whisk for 30 seconds to evenly mix. Pour the apple cider and buttermilk into a large measuring cup and add the vanilla. Stir them together.

In a second large mixing bowl, combine the butter, brown sugar and granulated sugar. Beat them with an electric mixer on medium-high speed until light and fluffy, 3 to 4 minutes. Crack the eggs into a small bowl to check for shells. Add them to the butter mixture and beat them until just combined.

Add HALF of the flour mixture to the butter mixture and beat it on low speed until combined. Add HALF of the cider mixture and beat it on low speed until combined. Repeat with the remaining flour and cider mixture.

Pour the batter into a large resealable plastic bag. Seal the bag and snip off a small corner with scissors. Pipe the batter into the prepared donut wells so each well is two-thirds full. Bake for 15 to 18 minutes, or until the donuts bounce back when gently pressed.

While the donuts are baking, prepare the topping. Place the butter in a microwave-safe bowl and heat it for 30 seconds on HIGH, or until melted. Mix together the sugar and cinnamon in a shallow bowl.

Remove the donuts from the oven and turn them out onto a wire rack. Place the rack over a large piece of parchment paper. Brush each donut with the melted butter, using a pastry brush, or carefully drizzle and spread it with a spoon. Then, dip the top of each donut in the cinnamon-sugar.

Let the donuts dry for 10 minutes before serving.

GINORMOUS ELEGANT ELEPHANT EARS

**YIELD:
4 DOZEN COOKIES**

Want to knock Grandma's socks off this Thanksgiving? Surprise her with a pretty platter of these elegant and amazing elephant ear cookies. She'll be certain you had to take a special baking class to make them, but it will be just our secret that they only need just a few ingredients! They are perfect for a fancy-schmancy holiday tea, too.

2 cups (400 g) sugar, divided
1 tsp ground cinnamon
⅛ tsp kosher salt
2 sheets frozen puff pastry, defrosted according to package directions

Preheat the oven to 425°F (220°C, or gas mark 7). Set out two cookie pans and line them with parchment paper; set aside.

In a small bowl, combine half the sugar, cinnamon and salt and stir them together with a fork.

Pour the remaining 1 cup (200 g) of the sugar onto a large cutting board. Work with one puff pastry sheet at a time. Be sure you don't let the pastry thaw for too long, or it will become too soft and difficult to work with. If this happens, put it back in the fridge to chill. Unfold the first pastry sheet and lay it onto the sugar. Pour HALF of the remaining sugar mixture on top and use your fingers to spread it evenly over the top.

Use a rolling pin to lightly roll the dough until it is a 13-inch (33-cm) square and the sugar is pressed into the puff pastry.

Fold the sides of the square toward the center so the edges meet in the middle. Fold the outside edges in toward the middle a second time. Then, fold one side over the other as you would close a book. (See pictures for reference.)

Now you have a long rolled log of dough with six layers. Carefully slice the dough with a paring knife into ⅜-inch (1-cm) slices. Place each, cut side up, on a prepared cookie pan.

Repeat with the second sheet of puff pastry, the remaining sugar on the cutting board and the second prepared pan.

Bake the elephant ears for 6 minutes, or until the sugar has caramelized and looks golden brown. Remove the pans from the oven, using your oven mitts. Carefully flip each cookie over with a spatula and bake for another 3 to 5 minutes. When they are golden brown on both sides, transfer the cookies to a wire rack to cool.

NOTE: Watch carefully; the cookies can burn quickly if left unattended. The cookies will bake faster as the dough becomes warmer.

Fold the puff pastry in towards the center on both sides.

Fold one side in towards the center again.

Repeat with the other side. Both ends should be touching in the middle.

Fold the pastry over like you're closing a book.

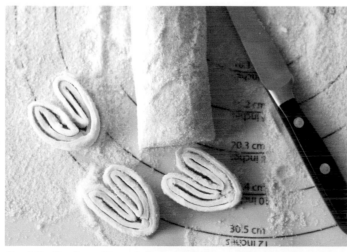

Carefully slice the cookies and place cut side down on the cookie sheet.

Bake until lightly golden.

MAPLE-SPICED PUMPKIN PIE

YIELD: 8 SERVINGS

Take the very best fall flavors, roll them all together and you have this drool-worthy maple-spiced pumpkin pie. Although it would be just perfect for your Thanksgiving table, you can spoil your family all season long with this special treat. Make any weekend better with this sweet and spiced classic dessert. Use your favorite cookie cutter shapes to make it all your own.

1 (14.1-oz [400-g]) package refrigerated piecrust

1 (15-oz [425-g]) can pure pumpkin puree

2 tbsp (15 g) all-purpose flour, plus more for dusting

½ tsp ground cinnamon

½ tsp ground nutmeg

½ tsp ground ginger

1 tbsp (14 g) salted butter, softened

1 cup (200 g) sugar

1 cup (237 ml) milk

2 tbsp (30 ml) maple syrup

2 large eggs

Homemade Whipped Cream (page 28), or 1 (13-oz [370-g]) store-bought canister, for serving (optional)

Preheat the oven to 425°F (220°C, or gas mark 7). Set out a 9-inch (23-cm) pie plate. Open the rolls of piecrust and set them on your counter to warm up a bit while you prepare the pie filling.

In your large mixing bowl, combine the pumpkin, flour, cinnamon, nutmeg, ginger, butter, sugar, milk and maple syrup. Crack the eggs into a small bowl and check for shells. Add the eggs to the pumpkin mixture and stir everything together until smooth.

Roll open one of the piecrusts and gently place it in the pie plate. Smooth the crust along the bottom of the plate and up the walls of the dish. Use your fingers to gently crimp the edge of the crust. Take a fork and prick the bottom of the piecrust a few times over the entire bottom of the plate. This will help prevent crust bubbles from forming.

Pour the prepared pie filling into the piecrust and smooth it out evenly.

Sprinkle a spoonful of flour on a cutting board and unroll the second piecrust. Use tiny cookie cutters to cut decorative shapes from the crust and place them along the edge of the pie.

Place the pie on a cookie pan to help prevent spills in the oven. Bake the pie for 15 minutes.

Lower the oven heat to 350°F (175°C, or gas mark 4) and then continue to bake the pie for 20 minutes. Remove the pie from the oven and wrap aluminum foil around the edges of the pan to cover up the decorative crust so it doesn't burn. Carefully place the pie back in the oven and bake for another 25 to 30 minutes. You will know the pie is done when a knife inserted in the center comes out clean. Remove from the oven and let cool in its pan.

Serve cooled to room temperature or chilled from the fridge with whipped cream, if desired.

THANKFUL-FOR-YOU CAKE POP BOUQUET

**YIELD:
30 TO 34 POPS**

Flowers put a smile on anyone's face when you give them with gratitude. If you want to go the extra step and make them beam with joy, thank them with these dainty and delectable daisy pops. Don't forget a sweet and simple handwritten note to tell them why they matter to you.

1 package 4-inch (10-cm)-long lollipop or cake pop sticks

1 (9 x 13–inch [23 x 33–cm]) sheet cake (page 57), prepared without chocolate chips, or 1 (15.2-oz [432-g]) box vanilla cake mix, baked according to package directions

1 cup (256 g) Sweet Buttercream or Cream Cheese Frosting (page 38 or 42) or ½ (16-oz [455-g]) canister prepared vanilla frosting

3 (10-oz [280-g]) packages candy melts

2 (0.33-oz [9.6-g]) boxes floral candy decorations

Set out the package of lollipop or cake pop sticks.

Prepare the cake and allow it to cool completely. Put the cooled cake in your large mixing bowl. Use clean hands to break it up into small crumbs. Add the frosting and stir it into the cake crumbs with a spoon or spatula. Chill the dough for 30 minutes.

Set out a cookie pan and line it with parchment paper. Use a spoon to scoop the dough into 1-inch (2.5-cm) balls. Roll the cake balls in your hands to make them perfectly round. Line them up on the parchment paper. Chill the cake balls in the fridge for 1 hour.

Once it is melted, the candy coating will thicken as it cools, so be sure to work with just one bag at a time. Transfer one bag's worth of the candy melts to a microwave-safe bowl. Heat them on HIGH for 20 seconds. Use oven mitts to remove the bowl and then stir. Continue to heat in 20-second sessions at a time, stirring in between, until the candy is melted and smooth.

Place one lollipop stick into each of the cake balls. Holding a cake pop by the stick, dip it at an angle (not straight down) into the melted candy coating. Swirl and lift it back out of the coating at an upward angle. If you dip it straight up and down, the cake ball will likely fall off the stick. If the candy coating starts to thicken, you can use a spoon to help spread it over the cake ball.

Add the candy floral decorations to the still-wet cake pop. Prop up the cake pop in a heavy drinking glass to finish drying. Repeat to coat and decorate the remaining cake pops.

If your cake pops are slipping down the stick, you can let them dry and harden while lying flat on parchment paper. The dried candy coating will help them stay on the stick better.

Thankful

SMART COOKIES

Hey, smarty pants! Kick off the new school year with a fresh start and these delicious sweet lunch box treats. Did you know that oatmeal helps boost your brain power? Bundle a batch up to share with your friends at the bus stop or enjoy them for an extra-sweet after-school snack.

1 cup (125 g) all-purpose flour

¾ tsp baking powder

½ tsp baking soda

½ tsp salt

14 tbsp (1¾ sticks [197 g]) salted butter

1 cup (200 g) granulated sugar

¼ cup (60 g) packed light brown sugar

1 large egg

1 tsp vanilla extract

2½ cups (200 g) old-fashioned rolled oats

½ cup (55 g) chopped pecans

½ cup (43 g) sweetened coconut flakes

Preheat the oven to 350°F (175°C, or gas mark 4). Set out a cookie pan and line it with parchment paper; set aside.

In a medium bowl, whisk together the flour, baking powder, baking soda and salt.

In your large mixing bowl, cream the butter, granulated sugar and brown sugar together until light and fluffy. Scrape down the sides of the bowl. Crack the egg into a small bowl. Then add the egg and vanilla to the butter and sugar mixture. Beat with an electric mixer on medium-low speed until just mixed, about 30 seconds. Stop the mixer and scrape the bowl. Add the flour mixture. Mix until just barely incorporated. Gradually add the oats and mix until well combined.

If the store-bought chopped pecans are still too big for your taste, you can finely chop them in a food processor. They add fantastic crunch to the cookies. Stir in the chopped pecans and coconut.

Scoop out 2-tablespoon (30-g) mounds of dough and roll them into balls. Arrange only eight balls per pan since they really spread out. Lightly flatten the cookies and then gently press a fingerprint in the center to help them cook evenly.

Bake one pan at a time until the cookies are golden brown, their edges are crisp and their centers are slightly soft, 13 to 16 minutes.

Remove from the oven. Cooling on the cookie pan will make them extra crispy.

STRAWBERRY PRETZEL CHEESECAKE BARS

YIELD: 12 BARS

Want to make family game night extra special? These sweet and salty treats might just give you the leading edge in the game. Your family will be so distracted by the deliciousness, you can sneak your winning moves before they notice!

CRUST

2½ cups (160 g) pretzels, plus ½ cup (32 g) for garnish

¼ cup (60 g) light brown sugar

12 tbsp (1½ sticks [167 g]) salted butter, melted

CHEESECAKE

16 oz (455 g) cream cheese, softened

1¼ cups (250 g) granulated sugar

¼ cup (60 g) sour cream

¼ cup (30 g) all-purpose flour

1½ tsp (8 ml) vanilla extract

2 large eggs

STRAWBERRY SWIRL TOPPING

1 cup (237 ml) strawberry jam sauce (page 44) or 1 cup (267 g) prepared strawberry pie filling (from a 21-oz [595-g] can)

Preheat the oven to 350°F (175°C, or gas mark 4).

Place the 2½ cups (160 g) of pretzels inside a large resealable plastic bag and seal the bag. Use a rolling pin to crush the pretzels into fine crumbs.

Transfer the pretzel crumbs to a medium bowl and add the brown sugar. Stir to combine. Pour in the melted butter and stir until the crumbs are all moistened with butter.

Pour the pretzel mixture into a 9 x 13–inch (23 x 33–cm) baking dish. Firmly press the crumbs with your fingers to form an even crust in the bottom of the pan. Really pack in the pretzel mixture so that it forms a solid base layer. You can use the bottom of a measuring cup to press them even tighter. Bake the crust for 8 minutes and then let it sit on the stovetop while you prepare the filling.

To prepare the cheesecake, place the cream cheese in your large mixing bowl. Beat it with an electric mixer on medium speed for 1 minute. Add the granulated sugar, sour cream, flour and vanilla and beat them together until the mixture is smooth.

Crack the eggs into a small bowl to check for shell pieces. Add the eggs to the cream cheese mixture and beat until combined, 1 more minute. Pour the cheesecake filling evenly over the pretzel crust.

Add the strawberry topping. Gently spoon the strawberry jam or pie filling all around the top of the cheesecake, leaving white patches of filling showing through. Use a butter knife to swirl the filling into a pretty pattern over the top.

Bake for 35 minutes, or until the top doesn't jiggle when you gently wiggle the pan. Remove from the oven, let cool and then chill in the fridge for 2 to 3 hours before serving. Decorate the bars by pressing the ½ cup (32 g) of reserved pretzels into the top

Family

MARVELOUS MOVIE CANDY COOKIES

YIELD: 2 DOZEN

When that movie you've just been dying to see is finally ready to watch at home, pop the popcorn, grab your family and throw a movie party! For an extra-special surprise, turn M&M's, a classic movie candy, into a delicious couch-friendly cookie treat.

1 cup (125 g) all-purpose flour

¼ tsp baking soda

¼ tsp salt

6 tbsp (¾ stick [85 g]) salted butter, melted

½ cup (115 g) packed brown sugar

¼ cup (50 g) granulated sugar

1 large egg

1 tsp vanilla extract

½ cup (100 g) mini M&M's candies, plus more for topping

½ batch Sweet Buttercream Frosting (page 38) (optional)

Preheat the oven to 325°F (170°C, or gas mark 3). Set out two cookie pans and line them with parchment paper; set aside.

In a medium bowl, combine the flour, baking soda and salt and whisk together.

In your large mixing bowl, combine the butter, brown sugar and granulated sugar. Using an electric mixer, cream them until light and fluffy. Crack the egg into a small bowl. Add the vanilla and beat them into the butter mixture. Add the flour mixture to the bowl, and with your mixer on low speed, beat until the dough is just combined. Scrape the beaters to get the dough into the bowl and then use a spatula to stir in the M&M's. Don't beat them with the mixer, or it will crack your candies.

Use a tablespoon to scoop a portion of dough. Roll it into a ball with clean hands. Place a ball on a prepared cookie pan and gently press a few more M&M's into the top of the cookie for decoration. Repeat with the remaining dough.

Bake for 10 to 12 minutes, using oven mitts to carefully rotate your pans halfway through the baking. This will make the cookies brown evenly. The cookies should be soft and puffy with the edges just lightly browned.

The cookies are delicious all on their own, or for another special occasion, you can make little sandwiches out of them using a half-batch of Sweet Buttercream Frosting.

SCRUMP-TIOUS SNICKER-DOODLES

**YIELD:
2 DOZEN COOKIES**

Got a mini-break from school this fall? Spend the afternoon in the kitchen whipping up these classic buttery cookies. The cinnamon-sugar will warm you up from your head down to your toes. These make awesome Christmas cookies, too. The dough freezes well; you could make a batch of it now to bake during the holiday season!

3½ cups (438 g) all-purpose flour

½ tsp baking soda

½ tsp cream of tartar

½ lb (2 sticks [225 g]) salted butter, softened

2 cups (400 g) sugar

2 large eggs

¼ cup (59 ml) milk

1 tsp vanilla extract

TOPPING

3 tbsp (39 g) sugar

1 tsp ground cinnamon

In a medium bowl, combine the flour, baking soda and cream of tartar and whisk together.

In your large mixing bowl, combine the butter and sugar and beat them with an electric mixer on medium-high speed until light and fluffy. Crack the eggs into a small cup to check for shells. Add them to the butter mixture along with the milk and vanilla. Beat them together until just combined.

Pour the flour mixture into the butter mixture and beat them together until the dough is wet and combined. Cover the dough in plastic wrap and chill in your fridge for at least 1 hour.

To bake the cookies, preheat the oven to 375°F (190°C, or gas mark 5). Set out two cookie pans and line them with parchment paper.

Combine the sugar and cinnamon in a small bowl. Use a tablespoon to scoop the dough in 1-inch (2.5-cm) portions. Roll the dough into a ball shape and then roll it in the cinnamon-sugar mixture.

Place the cookie ball on the prepared cookie pans and use the bottom of a drinking glass to gently press and slightly flatten the dough. Repeat with the remaining dough, spacing the balls 2 to 3 inches (5 to 7.5 cm) apart.

Sprinkle the tops of the prepared cookies with a little more of the cinnamon-sugar mix and then bake them for 7 to 8 minutes. Be careful not to overbake them; the cookies should be soft and chewy.

Remove from the oven and let the cookies cool on the cookie pans for 1 to 2 minutes before transferring them to a wire rack to cool completely.

FALL COLOR COOKIES

YIELD: 3 DOZEN

Capture the season of leaves bursting with color and falling all around you in these crispy chocolate cookies. They are a delightful dessert for any fall festivities you have planned.

½ lb (2 sticks [225 g]) salted butter, softened

1 cup (225 g) packed light brown sugar

1 cup (200 g) granulated sugar

2 tsp (10 ml) vanilla extract

2 large eggs, at room temperature

⅔ cup (74 g) unsweetened cocoa powder

2 cups (250 g) all-purpose flour

1 tsp baking soda

1 tsp kosher salt

2 (10.5-oz [298-g]) bags Reese's Pieces, divided

Preheat the oven to 350°F (175°C, or gas mark 4). Set out a cookie pan and line it with parchment paper; set aside.

In your large mixing bowl, combine the butter, brown sugar and granulated sugar. Beat them with an electric mixer on medium-high speed until the butter is light and fluffy. Stop the mixer and scrape the bowl. Add the vanilla. Working with one egg at a time, crack the egg into a small bowl and then add it to the mixer. Beat it into the dough and then add the next egg. Beat until just combined.

Add the cocoa powder and mix again, starting slowly because the powder will poof and spill onto your counter if you go too fast. Scrape the bowl.

In a medium bowl, combine the flour, baking soda and salt and stir together. Add the flour mixture to the chocolate mixture and mix on low speed until it is just combined. Scrape the beaters and the bowl to get all the dough together and then use a spoon to stir in 2 cups (400 g) of the Reese's Pieces. Don't beat them, or your candies will get crushed. Set aside the leftover candies.

Scoop large rounded tablespoons of dough and place them 2 to 3 inches (5 to 7.5 cm) apart on the prepared cookie pan. Dampen your clean hands and flatten the dough slightly. Press the remaining candies into the top of the cookies for decoration.

Bake for exactly 15 minutes (the cookies will still be soft and seem under-done). Remove from the oven and let the cookies cool slightly on the pan. After 5 minutes, transfer the cookies to a wire rack to cool completely.

NOTE: Both the baked cookies and the raw dough can be stored in the freezer, if you'd like to prepare the treat ahead of time.

WITCH'S CAULDRON BROWNIE BITES

**YIELD:
12 BROWNIE BITES**

Need to stir up a spooky treat for your Halloween party? These decadent brownie bites are topped with a wickedly delicious buttercream swirl and edible potion bubbles. Your friends will love scooping up the frosting with the salty witch's broom handle topper.

BROWNIES
Baking spray, for pan
2 oz (55 g) unsweetened baking chocolate
2 oz (55 g) semisweet baking chocolate
12 tbsp (1½ sticks [167 g]) salted butter
1¾ cups (350 g) sugar
1 tbsp (15 ml) vanilla extract
2 tbsp (14 g) unsweetened cocoa powder
3 large eggs
1 cup (125 g) all-purpose flour
½ tsp salt

DECORATION
1 batch Sweet Buttercream Frosting (page 38)
Green food gel
Assorted edible sprinkles
12 pretzel sticks

Preheat the oven to 350°F (175°C, or gas mark 4). Spray each well of a 12-muffin tin with baking spray and set aside.

Set out a large, microwave-safe bowl. Break the baking chocolate portions into smaller pieces, using clean hands, and place them in the bowl. If the chocolate is too hard to break, you can place it in a resealable plastic bag and break it with a kitchen mallet.

Cut the butter into small chunks with a butter knife and add it to the bowl of chocolate. Heat the chocolate and butter on HIGH power for 30 seconds. Use oven mitts to remove the bowl and carefully stir it with a cooking spoon. Continue to heat and stir the chocolate mixture for 30-second sessions, stirring in between until the chocolate is melted and smooth.

Stir the sugar into the chocolate mixture until smooth. Add the vanilla and cocoa powder and stir. Crack the eggs into a small bowl to check for shells. Lightly whisk the eggs and then pour them into the chocolate mixture. Stir until evenly combined. Add the flour and salt and stir until just combined.

Evenly divide the brownie batter among the prepared muffin wells. Wipe up any splatters from the top of the tin. Bake the brownies for 15 minutes, or until a toothpick inserted into the middle of a brownie comes out clean.

Remove from the oven and let the brownies cool completely in the muffin tin, then carefully remove them and place on a clean cookie pan for decorating.

To decorate, tint the buttercream green by stirring in three or four drops of green food gel. Transfer the buttercream to a pastry bag and top each brownie with a swirl of spooky frosting. Sprinkle a mixture of sprinkles over the top and decorate with a pretzel stick for the broom handle. It's okay to poke the tip of the pretzel into the top of the brownie so it doesn't fall over in the frosting.

Hocus POCUS

CHOCOLATE EYEBALL TRUFFLES

**YIELD:
18 TRUFFLES**

Your friends won't be able to stop staring at these ghostly cookies that stare right back! The best part? Just how many eyes they have is all up to you! Combine different sizes for even more personality.

1 (8-oz [225-g]) package cream cheese
1 (20-oz [560-g]) package chocolate sandwich cookies, such as Oreos
1 (10-oz [280-g]) bag white chocolate melts
Candy eye decorations

Place the container of cream cheese on your counter and let it come to room temperature for 1 hour before you begin.

Place all the cookies in a large resealable plastic bag. Seal the bag and crush them, using a kitchen mallet or rolling pin. When all the cookies have been broken into small crumbs, transfer them to your large mixing bowl along with the softened cream cheese. Use an electric mixer on medium speed to blend the cookies into the cream cheese. When the mixture has formed a large ball of dough, place it in the refrigerator to chill for 15 minutes.

Set out a cookie pan and line it with parchment paper. You will form the truffle balls and store them here. Using clean hands, pinch off some of the chilled dough and roll it into balls about 1¼ inches (3 cm) in diameter. (Not too big, not too small!) Place them on the prepared pan. When all the balls have been formed, place the cookie pan back into the fridge to chill while you prepare the coating.

Transfer the white chocolate melts to a microwave-safe bowl. Heat on HIGH for 30 seconds and then use oven mitts to remove the bowl and stir the candy. Continue to heat in 15-second sessions, stirring in between until melted and smooth.

Once the candy is smooth and creamy, take your chilled dough balls and use a spoon to roll each ball, one at a time, in the melted candy to coat. Gently drain off the excess candy coating before placing the covered truffle right back on the cookie pan.

You can drizzle more candy coating over the truffles to mimic a mummy's wrappings or immediately add the googly candy eyes for decoration. Once all the truffle balls have been coated and decorated, allow them to completely dry and harden in the fridge.

CANDY CORN FUDGE

YIELD: 15 SQUARES OF FUDGE

This swirly sweet surprise will astonish your neighbors when you Boo their house this Halloween. Easy to make but utterly impressive, who wouldn't want to discover this on their doorstep one evening? Don't forget the "You've been Boo'd" note so they know to pay it forward.

1 tbsp (14 g) salted butter
¼ cup (59 ml) heavy whipping cream
1½ tsp (8 ml) vanilla extract
2½ cups (238 g) white chocolate melts
1 (22-oz [624-g]) bag candy corn
Assorted sprinkles

Set out a 9-inch (23-cm) square baking dish and line it with parchment paper; set aside.

Use a butter knife to cut the butter into smaller chunks and place it in a medium microwave-safe bowl. Pour in the cream and vanilla. Stir to coat the butter with the cream. Heat on high for 40 seconds, or until the butter has completely melted and the liquid is hot. Use oven mitts to remove the bowl and stir the mixture carefully.

Stir in the white chocolate melts and let the heat of the liquid melt them. If they don't melt all the way, microwave the mixture on HIGH in 10-second sessions until smooth.

Spread the fudge batter in the prepared baking dish and press the candy corn evenly over the top of the fudge. Sprinkle the sprinkles over the top and gently press them into the fudge as well.

Let the fudge cool and harden. You can remove it from the dish by pulling up the parchment paper. Place the fudge on a cutting board. Cut the fudge squares with a butter knife.

WINTER ❄
festivities

Winter is the very best time for baking, don't you think? Take chilly weather outside and add it to a string of warm holidays that bring friends and family together to celebrate the end of the year and you've got the perfect recipe for sweet desserts.

Having a cookie exchange party with your friends? Don't miss the chocolate Crinkle Cookies (page 163) or our sweet little Spritz Cookies (page 164). Need a glitzy treat for a special occasion? Your family will love the Sticky Pudding Trifle Parfaits (page 168) and the orange-chocolate Sparkle Cupcakes (page 172). Need a homemade gift for your teacher or your neighbors? Try our sweet Candy Cane Heart Pops (page 160).

The classic Gingerbread Cookie Cutouts (page 159) will go great with a mug of hot cocoa. Enjoy Red Velvet Donuts with Cream Cheese Glaze (page 156) before you open your gifts on Christmas morning. And the sparkly Brownie Ball Drop Pops (page 175) are perfect for counting down to the New Year!

No matter what you're celebrating this winter, we've got a recipe for you.

RED VELVET DONUTS WITH CREAM CHEESE GLAZE

**YIELD:
12 DONUTS**

Prepare a batch of these pretty red velvet donuts for Christmas morning. They make a quick breakfast before you launch into opening your gifts from Santa. For an added flair, decorate them with sweet sprinkles.

Baking spray, for pans
1¼ cups (156 g) all-purpose flour
½ tsp baking soda
½ tsp salt
1½ tsp (4 g) unsweetened cocoa powder
¾ cup (150 g) granulated sugar
1 large egg
½ cup (118 ml) buttermilk
½ cup (118 ml) canola oil
½ tsp vanilla extract
½ tsp vinegar
1 tbsp (15 ml) red food coloring

CREAM CHEESE GLAZE
3 oz (85 g) cream cheese
2 cups (240 g) powdered sugar
1 tsp vanilla extract
Splash of milk

Sprinkles (optional)

Preheat the oven to 350°F (175°C, or gas mark 4). Spray the wells of two donut pans with baking spray and set aside.

In your large mixing bowl, combine the flour, baking soda, salt, cocoa powder and granulated sugar. Whisk them together and set aside.

Crack the egg into a medium bowl and check for shells. Add the buttermilk, canola oil, vanilla, vinegar and food coloring and whisk together.

Slowly pour the buttermilk mixture into the flour mixture and whisk them together until all the clumps are gone. The batter will be wet and heavy. If the batter isn't red enough, you can add a few more drops of food coloring and stir them in. Just remember to add a little at a time.

Transfer the batter to a large liquid measuring cup with a spout. Pour the batter into the prepared donut wells, filling each about half full. Use a spoon or toothpick to even out the batter, if needed.

Bake for 10 to 12 minutes. Remove from the oven and let the donuts cool in the pan for 5 minutes before carefully transferring them to a wire rack.

While the donuts are baking and cooling, prepare the glaze. In a medium bowl, combine the cream cheese, powdered sugar and vanilla. Beat them together with an electric mixer on medium speed until smooth and fluffy. Add a splash of milk, if needed, to make the glaze a little easier to spread.

When the donuts are completely cool, frost them with the glaze. You can spread it on with a knife or pour the glaze into a resealable plastic bag and snip a corner with scissors to drizzle the glaze over the tops of the donuts. Add the sprinkles (if using) while the glaze is still wet.

GINGER-BREAD COOKIE CUTOUTS

YIELD: 108 SMALL TO MEDIUM-SIZE COOKIES

This classic Christmas cookie is delicious with just a sprinkle of powdered sugar, but you could also frost them with buttercream or cream cheese frosting and holiday candies. They tend to puff up a little but still retain their form, so they are perfect for any cookie cutter shape you love. Why not spell out a merry greeting in letters for your family? This dough makes a very large amount of cookies. You can easily divide the dough in half and freeze some for another day if you don't want to bake them all at once.

½ lb (2 sticks [225 g]) salted butter, softened

1 cup (200 g) sugar

2 large eggs

1¼ cups (296 ml) molasses

1 tsp vanilla extract

5½ cups (688 g) all-purpose flour, plus more for dusting

1½ tsp (7 g) baking soda

1 tsp salt

2 tsp (4 g) ground ginger

1 tbsp (7 g) ground cinnamon

1½ tsp (3 g) ground cloves

2 tsp (4 g) ground nutmeg

OPTIONAL DECORATIONS

Vanilla Cookie Glaze (page 43)

Cream Cheese Frosting (page 42)

Sprinkles or hot cinnamon candies

In your large mixing bowl, combine the butter and sugar and beat with an electric mixer on high speed until light and fluffy. Crack the eggs into a small bowl to check for shells. Add the molasses, eggs and vanilla to the butter mixture and stir them in until light and fluffy.

In a large bowl, combine the flour, baking soda, salt, ginger, cinnamon, cloves and nutmeg. Whisk them together. Add the flour mixture to the butter mixture a little at a time, beating it on medium speed to mix them well.

Divide the dough into three smaller portions. Cover each with plastic wrap and chill in the fridge for 1 hour or overnight.

Preheat the oven to 375°F (190°C, or gas mark 5). Set out two cookie pans and line them with parchment paper.

Sprinkle some flour onto your working surface and working with one portion of dough at a time, roll it out to ¼-inch (6-mm) thickness. Cut the cookies to your desired shape, dipping the cutters in flour if they are sticking. Carefully transfer the cookies to the prepared cookie pans.

Bake for 6 to 7 minutes for medium-size cookies. Remove from the oven and let the cookies cool on the cookie pans for 5 minutes, then transfer to a wire rack.

You can use a batch of the colorful cookie glaze to frost your shapes, but we really love these cookies with a schmear of cream cheese frosting. You could add sprinkles or hot cinnamon candies for a festive twist.

CANDY CANE HEART POPS

**YIELD:
12 POPS**

These adorable lovey-dovey little pops are sure to warm the hearts of everyone you share them with. They are easy to make and look sweet gathered like a bouquet in a jar with a bow.

12 lollipop or cake pop sticks
24 mini candy canes
1 (12-oz [340-g]) package candy melts
Sprinkles (optional)

Lay a large piece of waxed or parchment paper on your counter. Set out the lollipop or cake pop sticks.

Pair up two mini candy canes to form each heart. Place a lollipop stick inside the bottom of each heart with the tips of the candy canes touching the stick.

In a microwave-safe bowl, add the candy melts. Heat on HIGH for 30 seconds. Wear oven mitts to remove the bowl for stirring. Heat in 15-second sessions more as needed to get the candy to completely melt and stir smoothly. Really stir a lot each time; it will help the candy become smooth with the least amount of heat.

Carefully spoon the melted candy into each heart. Start with just a little and add more if you need to fill it. You might want to use a toothpick or the tip of your spoon to help push the candy filling all around inside the heart.

Give the candy filling 1 minute to begin to set and then add your sprinkles, if using, while it is still wet.

Let the hearts completely cool and then gently peel them away from the paper to serve.

HO HO HO!

CRINKLE COOKIES

**YIELD:
28 TO 30 COOKIES**

If you need a festive cookie that doesn't require cookie cutters, these crinkle cookies are just perfect for a holiday treat tray. They look frosted and snowy, but are sweet and fudgy inside.

1 cup (125 g) all-purpose flour

½ cup (55 g) unsweetened cocoa powder

1 tsp baking powder

¼ tsp baking soda

½ tsp salt

3 large eggs

1½ cups (338 g) packed light brown sugar

1 tsp vanilla extract

4 oz (225 g) unsweetened baking chocolate

4 tbsp (½ stick [55 g]) salted butter

COATING

½ cup (100 g) granulated sugar

½ cup (60 g) powdered sugar

Preheat the oven to 325°F (170°C, or gas mark 3). Set out two cookie pans and line them with parchment paper; set aside.

In a medium bowl, combine the flour, cocoa powder, baking powder, baking soda and salt. Whisk them together.

Crack the eggs into your large mixing bowl and look for shells. Add the brown sugar and vanilla. Beat together on medium speed until combined.

Break up the chocolate into small pieces by placing it in a resealable plastic bag and hitting it with a kitchen mallet. Place the chocolate and butter in a microwave-safe bowl. Heat on HIGH in 30-second sessions, stirring in between, until just melted. Use oven mitts to remove the bowl from the microwave. Slowly pour the melted chocolate into the egg mixture, whisking the whole time.

Once the chocolate is mixed in, stir in the flour mixture. Be sure to scrape the bowl and check for hidden pockets of dry flour. Let the dough sit for 10 minutes.

Next, coat the cookies. Set up your cookie assembly line by placing the granulated sugar on a clean pie plate. Then, place the powdered sugar on a separate pie plate or dish.

Pinch portions of dough and roll them into 2-inch (5-cm) balls. Drop each ball first into the granulated sugar and roll it around to coat it completely. Then, roll the cookie ball in the powdered sugar to coat and place on the prepared cookie pan. Place the cookies 3 inches (7.5 cm) apart on the pans.

Bake the cookies, just one pan at a time, for 8 to 10 minutes. They will puff and crackle around the edges and seem too soft in the center, but you don't want to overbake them. Remove from the oven and let them cool on the pan for 5 minutes before transferring to a wire rack to cool completely.

SPRITZ COOKIES

**YIELD:
95 COOKIES**

Shooting cookies from a cookie press? Yes, please! I'm not sure there are any cookies quite as fun to make as these. Although they look fancy and complicated, they are one of the easiest cookies ever! The delicate buttery base is the perfect palette for playing with sprinkles and chocolate to your heart's content. Don't have a cookie press? No worries; you can turn them into thumbprint cookies, too.

½ lb (2 sticks [225 g]) salted butter, softened

1¼ cups (150 g) powdered sugar

½ tsp salt

1 large egg

1 tsp vanilla extract

½ tsp almond extract

2½ cups (313 g) all-purpose flour

GLAZE

1 cup (120 g) powdered sugar

½ tsp vanilla extract

2 to 3 tbsp (30 to 45 ml) water

OPTIONAL DECORATIONS

Assorted sprinkles

Melted chocolate

Preheat the oven to 375°F (190°C, or gas mark 5). Place a wire rack on a piece of parchment paper and set aside.

In your large mixing bowl, combine the butter, powdered sugar and salt. Beat with an electric mixer on low speed until just combined and then continue to beat on medium-high speed until light and fluffy. Stop the mixer and scrape the bowl as needed.

Crack the egg into a small bowl to check for shells. Add the vanilla and almond extracts to the egg. Gently whisk with a fork to break up the yolk and combine the extracts with the egg. Pour the egg mixture into the butter mixture and beat until just combined. The batter will appear slightly curdled, not smooth.

Add the flour to the butter mixture and beat until just combined.

Spoon the dough into a cookie press fitted with the decorative disk of your choice. Press the cookies 2 inches (5 cm) apart directly onto a cookie pan. Bake for 6 to 8 minutes; the cookies should be firm but not browned. Remove from the oven and transfer the cookies to the wire rack.

For the glaze, in a small bowl, combine the powdered sugar, vanilla and 2 tablespoons (30 ml) of the water. Gently stir to form a glaze. If the mixture is too thick, add another tablespoon (15 ml) of water. You can either drizzle the glaze over the cooled cookies or dip them right into the glaze. Before the glaze sets, sprinkle the sprinkles over the top, if using.

You can also dip the cookies into melted chocolate. They look pretty completely covered or half-dipped. Add sprinkles while the chocolate is still wet.

NOTE: Don't have a cookie press? Roll the cookies into balls with clean hands and then gently press your thumb in the top to make a thumbprint cookie. Once they are baked, you can fill the thumbprint with melted chocolate or Sweet and Smooth Strawberry Jam Sauce (page 44).

REINDEER MUNCH

**YIELD:
12 SERVINGS**

When you need an extra-special snack for your family's Christmas movie marathon, nothing beats this sweet and salty popcorn mix. It makes a sweet treat for bundling up for your friends during the holiday season, too. Wrap it in clear bags with pretty ribbons for a homemade gift they'll adore.

3 cups (30 g) popped popcorn

4 cups (108 g) Rice Chex cereal or similar product

1 cup (64 g) pretzel twists

½ cup (70 g) roasted cashews

⅔ cup (173 g) peanut butter or your favorite nut or seed butter

3 tbsp (42 g) salted butter

2 to 3 tbsp (20 to 30 g) holiday sprinkles

2 cups (240 g) powdered sugar

¾ cup (150 g) red and green M&M's

Place the popcorn, cereal, pretzels and cashews into a gallon-size (3.8-L) resealable plastic bag. Set aside.

Place the peanut butter and butter in a microwave-safe bowl. Heat on HIGH for 20 seconds and use oven mitts to remove the bowl for stirring. Continue to heat in 20-second sessions and stir until the mixture is melted and smooth.

Pour the peanut butter mixture over the popcorn mixture, seal the bag and gently shake to coat everything in peanut butter.

Open the bag and add a few tablespoons (20 to 30 g) of sprinkles, seal the bag and shake again.

Open the bag and add the powdered sugar, seal the bag and shake again.

Pour the snack mixture into a serving bowl and gently stir in the M&M's.

STICKY PUDDING TRIFLE PARFAITS

YIELD: 8 PARFAITS

While not exactly traditional, we far prefer our twist on the Christmas classic sticky pudding. We kept the toffee flavor and added chopped-up brownies for a festive trifle your family will love.

1 batch brownies (page 76), or 1 (18.3-oz [519-g]) box brownie mix, prepared according to directions on package in a 9 x 13–inch (23 x 33–cm) baking pan

2 cups (475 ml) cold milk

2 (3.3-oz [94-g]) boxes pudding mix (vanilla, cheesecake or white chocolate flavor)

1 (8-oz [225-g]) container frozen whipped topping, thawed, divided

1 (17-oz [482-g]) bottle prepared caramel sauce

1 (8-oz [226-g]) package chopped toffee bits

Prepare the brownies and allow them to cool completely.

Meanwhile, prepare the filling. In your large mixing bowl, combine the milk and pudding mix. Beat them together on medium-high speed for 2 minutes. Stop the mixer and scrape the bowl as needed. Gently fold HALF of the whipped topping into the pudding mixture.

To assemble the trifles, cut the brownies into large chunks using a butter knife.

Set out eight individual parfait dishes. You can use pretty glasses or mason jars. Build the parfaits in layers. Start with a few spoonfuls of pudding, then the brownies, a drizzle of caramel and a sprinkle of chopped toffee, then repeat until the parfait dish is full. Top with dollops of whipped topping.

Chill the parfaits in the fridge for at least 1 hour before serving.

MINI MONKEY BREAD MUFFINS

YIELD: 12 MUFFINS

If your house is full of holiday guests, treat them to a special breakfast with these sweet and chewy mini monkey bread muffins. They take only minutes to prepare and are a huge hit with the family.

Baking spray, for pan
2 (8-count) cans prepared refrigerated cinnamon rolls
2 tsp (9 g) granulated sugar
2 tsp (5 g) ground cinnamon
8 tbsp (1 stick [112 g]) salted butter
3 tbsp (45 g) light brown sugar
Cream Cheese Glaze (page 156), or the frosting that comes with the rolls

Preheat the oven to 350°F (175°C, or gas mark 4). Spray the wells of a 12-muffin tin with baking spray and set aside.

Open the container of cinnamon rolls and separate each roll. Cut each into four pieces with a butter knife. Place the cubes of dough in a large resealable plastic bag. Add the granulated sugar and cinnamon to the bag and seal it closed. Gently shake the rolls in the cinnamon-sugar mixture until they are evenly coated.

Evenly distribute the dough among the prepared muffin wells. Don't pack them in too tightly; just gently fill each well.

Place the butter in a microwave-safe bowl and heat on HIGH for 40 seconds, or until melted. Remove with oven mitts. Stir in the brown sugar until the mixture is smooth. Use a spoon to pour the butter mixture over the dough in each well.

Bake for 18 minutes, or until golden brown. Remove from the oven and let the monkey breads cool in the muffin tin for 2 minutes.

For the glaze, you can use the cream cheese glaze recipe from the Red Velvet Donuts (page 156) or keep it extra easy and use the frosting that comes with the rolls. Stir the glaze with a butter knife and spread it evenly over the top of each muffin. Let the glaze set for a minute. Then, use a fork or spoon to gently lift the muffins out of the pan and onto a plate for serving.

SPARKLE CUPCAKES

**YIELD:
12 CUPCAKES**

This season is all about glitter and shine. We love to mix bright and zesty orange with rich and fudgy chocolate during the holidays. Top these festive cupcakes with edible sparkles for a glitzy treat just perfect for a Christmas Eve or New Year's Eve bash.

1½ cups (188 g) all-purpose flour

1 tsp baking powder

¼ tsp salt

8 tbsp (1 stick [112 g]) salted butter, softened

1 cup (200 g) sugar

3 large eggs

1 orange

1 tsp vanilla extract

½ cup (118 ml) milk

1 drop orange food coloring (optional)

½ cup (88 g) mini chocolate chips

Chocolate Fudge Frosting (page 41)

Sugar crystal sprinkles (optional)

Preheat the oven to 350°F (175°C, or gas mark 4). Line 12 wells of a muffin tin with a double layer of cupcake wrappers and set aside.

In a medium bowl, combine the flour, baking powder and salt and whisk them together.

In your large mixing bowl, combine the butter and sugar and beat them together with an electric mixer on medium-high speed until light and fluffy.

Crack the eggs into a small bowl to check for shells. Add the eggs to the butter mixture and mix them until just combined.

Wash and dry the orange. Use a Microplane zester to rub the orange and remove the orange zest. Microplanes can be very sharp, so you might want to ask an adult for help. Save the zest in a small bowl and set aside. Cut the orange in half and squeeze the juice into a bowl.

Add the vanilla, orange zest, 2 tablespoons (30 ml) of the orange juice and the milk to the butter mixture and mix for 30 seconds on low speed.

Slowly add the flour mixture and mix together until just combined. Gently stir in the food coloring, if you are using it. Fold in the mini chocolate chips.

Evenly divide the batter among the 12 prepared muffin wells until just over two-thirds full. Bake for 18 to 20 minutes, or until a toothpick inserted in the center of a cupcake comes out clean. Remove from the oven and let cool.

If you like, you can brush the remaining fresh orange juice over the top of the warm cupcakes, or mix 1 to 2 tablespoons (15 to 30 ml) of orange juice into the chocolate frosting for extra citrusy flavor.

Once cooled, frost with the chocolate fudge frosting using a butter knife. Then make them sparkle with a pinch of crystal sugar sprinkles.

SHIMMER

NEW YEAR'S EVE BROWNIE BALL DROP POPS

YIELD: 30 TO 34 BROWNIE POPS

3, 2, 1 . . . Happy New Year! These rich and fudgy brownie pops are the perfect way to say good-bye to the old year and hello to the new. Bright and shiny just like the famous countdown ball in New York City, they'll bring the sparkle to your end-of-year party.

1 batch brownies (page 76), or 1 (18.3-oz [159-g]) box brownie mix, prepared according to package directions

1 package of 4-inch (10-cm)-long lollipop or cake pop sticks

1 cup (256 g) Chocolate Fudge Frosting (page 41), or ½ (16-oz [455-g]) can prepared chocolate frosting

3 (12-oz [340-g]) packages candy melts

Silver edible star-shaped sprinkles

Prepare the brownies and allow them to cool completely. If you try to work with them while they are still warm, they will melt the frosting.

Set out a cookie pan and line it with waxed paper; set aside. Set out the lollipop or cake pop sticks.

Remove the brownies from the pan. Place the brownies in a large mixing bowl and use clean hands to break them up into smaller pieces. Add the frosting to the bowl and stir it into the brownies. Use your hands to work the frosting into the brownies to form a fudgy dough.

Use a tablespoon or small cookie scoop to form Ping-Pong ball–size portions of dough. Roll the dough into smooth balls with clean hands. Chill the brownie balls for 1 hour.

Once melted, the candy melts will begin to thicken as they cool, so be sure to work with just one bag of melts at a time. Place one bag's worth of the candy melts in a microwave-safe bowl and heat on HIGH for 30 seconds. Stir the candy melts and continue to heat in 30-second sessions until the candy is nice and smooth. Stir carefully after each burst of heat.

Prepare an assembly line with your brownie balls, the melted candy and the prepared cookie pan. Assemble the final brownie pops one pop at a time.

Stick a lollipop stick into the ball of dough and carefully dip it into the melted candy. Swirl and lift the ball of dough out of the melted candy at an angle and let it drip off into the bowl before setting it on the waxed paper–lined cookie pan, stick side up. Sprinkle the sprinkles over the pop while the candy coating is still wet.

Repeat for the remaining dough. If your melted candy starts to thicken too much, you can use a spoon to help spread it over the brownie ball.

CHOCOLATE SCOTCH-EROOS

YIELD: 24 BARS

You'll never forget the first treat you mastered making all by yourself. For my husband, it was these delicious and creamy peanut butter cereal bars covered in chocolate. He made them so often, he memorized the recipe. His mom always kept the ingredients in the pantry, so on a snowy day, he had just what he needed to make a special treat. We bet you will love them, too!

Baking spray, for pan and measuring cup
1 cup (200 g) sugar
1 cup (237 ml) light corn syrup
1 cup (260 g) peanut butter or your favorite nut or seed butter
6 cups (125 g) crisped rice cereal
1 cup (175 g) semisweet chocolate chips
1 cup (175 g) butterscotch chips

Spray a 9 x 13–inch (23 x 33–cm) baking dish with baking spray and set aside.

Find a BIG stockpot; you will be stirring the whole batch of cereal inside it. Measure and place the sugar in the pot. Then, spray the measuring cup with baking spray before you measure the corn syrup. It will be much easier to get it back out! Measure and add the corn syrup to the stockpot. Heat over medium heat, stirring with a spatula, until the sugar dissolves completely. When the mixture begins to boil, remove the pot from the heat.

Carefully stir in the peanut butter and mix well. Pour in the cereal and stir until it is well coated with the peanut butter mixture. The peanut butter will be very thick; use a long spoon to help, but it's okay to ask an adult, too.

Spread the cereal mixture into the prepared baking dish and press it evenly along the bottom. Let cool while you prepare the topping.

Place the chocolate and butterscotch chips in a microwave-safe bowl. Heat them on HIGH for 30 seconds and use oven mitts to remove them for stirring. Continue to heat in 30-second sessions until they are melted and smooth. They will melt better if you really stir, stir, stir between each session. Pour the mixture over the cooled cereal bars and spread evenly over the top.

Let the bars stand until the topping has cooled and firmed. Cut into bars and serve.

Snow
DAY!

SNOWBALL COOKIES

YIELD: 48 COOKIES

These white and puffy buttery cookies are perfect for snow day baking. They also happen to be my mom's all-time favorite Christmas cookie. She shapes them into crescent moons and calls them ladyfingers. You can have fun baking snowballs or surprise your mom or grandma with an elegant tea-time treat.

2 cups (220 g) chopped pecans
2 cups (240 g) powdered sugar
½ lb (2 sticks [225 g]) salted butter, softened
¼ cup (50 g) granulated sugar
1 tsp vanilla extract
2 cups (250 g) all-purpose flour

Preheat the oven to 325°F (170°C, or gas mark 3).

The chopped pecans need to be finely chopped. You can either put them in a food processor for a few spins or you can place them in a resealable plastic bag and break them up with a kitchen mallet. Set them aside.

Place the powdered sugar in a shallow bowl and set aside.

In your large mixing bowl, combine the butter and sugar and beat them with an electric mixer on medium-high speed until light and fluffy. Stop the mixer and scrape the bowl. Add the vanilla and beat it until well mixed in.

Add the flour and the pecans to the butter mixture and beat them in on low speed. Be sure to scrape the bowl once or twice. Once the flour is combined with the butter mixture, scrape the bowl and beaters.

Use a spoon to scoop 1-inch (2.5-cm) balls of dough. Roll them into round balls and place them 1 inch (2.5 cm) apart directly on a cookie pan. Bake for 16 to 18 minutes, or until lightly browned. Remove from the oven and let cool for 15 to 20 minutes before you roll them in the powdered sugar bowl, or the powdered sugar will melt and become gummy.

PARTY PRO

Now that you've baked your masterpiece, it is time to share it with your friends and family. After all that work of making it "just so," you wouldn't just want to plop it on the table and run. If you want to make your guests feel extra special, here's how to present your treat with love.

PARTY-PERFECT PRESENTATION IDEAS

- **PICK A PRETTY PLATE TO FIT YOUR TREAT:** Cookies look great piled neatly on a plate or platter or nestled into a treat tin lined with waxed paper. Cupcakes and bars are perfect for a pedestal cake plate. Snack mix treats and candies often work best inside a pretty bowl. Be sure to add a utensil for serving near the treat.

- **MAKE ROOM FOR MORE:** Party tables get crowded with food in a hurry. When you need more space, carefully stack two pedestal cake plates and arrange treats on both layers. This leaves more room for dishes from your friends and family on the table itself.

- **ANNOUNCE THE FLAVORS:** Get your guests excited about your treats by creating pretty table cards that explain the flavor of your treat. That way they know what to expect when they take a bite. This is a great place to make a note for friends with allergies if your recipe used peanuts or nuts.

PARTY ETIQUETTE FOR SERVING TREATS

THE BAKER TAKES THE LAST SERVING: Whether it is a cookie, cupcake or slice of cake, always cut the dessert and serve a piece to everyone else before you take one for yourself. The first piece should go to the guest of honor—either the birthday celebrant or most important person in the room. When in doubt, Grandma and Grandpa are always the most important.

DON'T TOUCH THE FOOD WITH YOUR HANDS: Before serving, be sure to wash your hands but don't touch the food directly with your fingers. Use a knife and spatula to cut and serve cakes or bars, or a napkin to pick up cookies.

OFFER THE SERVING WITH A FANCY NAPKIN AND A FORK OR SPOON, IF NEEDED: Make sure your guests have everything they need to enjoy the treat at the moment you give them their serving. It's not fun staring at a mouthwatering piece of cake but having no way to fork it into your mouth! Place the treat on a plate and offer it to your guest along with a napkin and fork or spoon, if needed.

HOW TO GIVE BAKED GOODIES AS GIFTS

Homemade treats are always appreciated and are a lovely way to show you care. If you want to give your goodie as a gift, remember these tricks:

- **PICK A TREAT THAT TRAVELS WELL:** Cookies, bars, snack mixes and candies make great gifts because they can get accidentally bumped a little in transit and not get broken or ruined. Treats with soft frosting, such as cupcakes, are a bit trickier.

- **CHOOSE THE RIGHT PACKAGING:** Plan to give your treat in a container that you don't expect to receive back. Your local craft store should offer several options, including clear plastic bags that can be tied with a pretty ribbon or colorful cardboard containers that are perfect for cookies or cupcakes.

- **LABEL YOUR TREAT:** Make a homemade tag with the name of the treat on it so your recipients know what they will be eating. This is another great place to add a note about potential allergies. Be sure to label your food if you used dairy, eggs, flour (gluten), peanuts or nuts.

10 WAYS TO CELEBRATE A HOLIDAY BEYOND FOOD

Baking for friends is a lovely way to celebrate the seasons, but there are plenty of ways to have fun beyond food, too! Any holiday or special occasion could be made even more fun with one of these creative party or activity ideas, whether you baked some treats or not.

1. Make a handwritten card or letter telling a friend or family member why they are special to you. Not sure what to say? Try one of these prompts:

    A. Write a character trait for each letter of their name.

    B. Make a top 10 list of your favorite memories with them.

    C. Draw a comic strip of something silly you did together.

2. Have a holiday crafting day and make something with your friends to decorate your rooms.

3. Host a random acts of kindness marathon.

4. Plan an epic game night, either board games or backyard games, depending on the weather.

5. Enjoy a spontaneous dance party in your living room with a seasonal playlist of your favorite tunes.

6. Dress with festive holiday accessories. Make your own hair clips or T-shirts with fun holiday sayings.

7. Take a photo walk around your neighborhood and look for signs of the season in the nature all around you that you can capture with a camera.

8. Watch your favorite holiday movie and make a list of all the best quotes.

9. Make a thoughtful homemade gift for your family; a coupon book is a great place to start.

10. Decorate the sidewalks in your neighborhood with festive messages in chalk.

BAKING SUBSTITUTIONS AND
HELPFUL MEASURING TRICKS

BAKING POWDER: You can replace 1 teaspoon of baking powder with ¼ teaspoon of baking soda plus ½ teaspoon of cream of tartar.

BAKING SODA: You can replace 1 teaspoon of baking soda with 1 tablespoon (14 g) of baking powder.

BROWN SUGAR: You can replace 1 cup (225 g) of brown sugar with 1 cup (200 g) of granulated sugar plus 2 tablespoons (30 ml) of molasses.

BUTTERMILK: You can replace 1 cup (237 ml) of buttermilk with 1 cup (237 ml) of milk plus 1 tablespoon (15 ml) of fresh lemon juice OR white vinegar. Stir the lemon juice or vinegar into the milk and let it sit for 5 minutes before using.

CAKE FLOUR: You can replace 1 cup (90 g) of cake flour with all-purpose flour and cornstarch: Measure 1 cup (125 g) of all-purpose flour and level it off. Then remove 2 tablespoons (15 g) of the flour. Put the flour in a small mixing bowl and add 2 tablespoons (16 g) of cornstarch. Whisk the flour and the cornstarch mixture together and then use in your recipe.

CHOCOLATE: You can replace 4 ounces (113 g) of an unsweetened solid chocolate bar with 4 tablespoons (½ stick [55 g]) of butter plus ⅔ cup (74 g) of unsweetened cocoa powder. Melt the butter in a microwave and stir in the chocolate powder. Use in place of the melted chocolate bar.

EGGS: You can replace one egg with ¼ cup (60 g) of applesauce. You can also try ½ of a banana mashed with ½ teaspoon of baking powder.

SOUR CREAM: You can replace 1 cup (230 g) of sour cream with 1 cup (230 g) of plain (unflavored) yogurt.

VEGETABLE OIL: You can replace 1 cup (237 ml) of vegetable oil with 1 cup (245 g) of applesauce.

HELPFUL MEASURING TIPS

1 tbsp = 3 tsp

¼ cup = 4 tbsp

⅓ cup = 5⅓ tbsp (5 tbsp + 1 tsp)

½ cup = 8 tbsp

¾ cup = 12 tbsp

THANK YOU!

At the heart of this book are all the loved ones I want to shower with treats.

The first tiny cookie I bake goes to Tori Demchuk: if it weren't for your special arrival in the world, this book would still be pure imagination.

A big batch of brownies goes to my editor, Sarah Monroe, for recognizing the hidden magic in a messy manuscript. I hope you'll share them with Meg Baskis, who designed a book straight out of my dreams. I'll be sure to send enough for the lunch room at Page Street Publishing so everyone who works so tirelessly to make this book a reality can have a well-deserved nibble.

A pretty batch of gluten-free candy cane heart pops needs to be made for my friend Carey Pace, for inspiring me with a fresh look for my food photography. Thanks for the boost of courage.

An ooey-gooey pan of S'mores Bars would definitely be devoured by the entire Harrington family. Zina, you've been taste-testing my baking experiments for over 16 years. Thank you for your amazing outlook that turns epic failures into delicious ice cream toppings.

I owe a pan of cheesecake bars to Michelle Malek for inspiring me with a constant rotation of ideas for holidays to celebrate. You show up ready to party, complete with coordinating party socks. I love you bunches.

My mom calls dibs on the next batch of Sunshine Bars, Dad needs Carrot Cake Donuts for his birthday and my sister Molly Tumanic will step right up and help me assemble some Sticky Pudding Trifles. Thank you for filling my childhood with amazing holiday memories so I can turn around and do the same for my girls.

Sophie and Charlotte, you get your pick: Will it be the Giant Birthday Cookie Cake or the Grasshopper Torte?! As much as I love baking treats for you, nothing tastes better than the ones you make for me. We three know, it's the love inside that makes it best. I'm the luckiest mom in the world because I get to celebrate all the things with you.

And the biggest, most Epic Chocolate Cake that shames all other cakes goes to my husband, Tim, the first person I ever baked a homemade (very wonky) birthday cake for and yet remains my biggest fan. Here's to a lifetime of amazing moments we get to celebrate together. I threw in the extra chocolate chips just for you.

ABOUT THE AUTHOR

Tiffany Dahle is a kitchen magician that can magnificently turn butter and eggs into towering cakes of awesome. Her stand mixer calls her kids to the kitchen Pied Piper–style. She's been baking with them since the time they could reach the counter with a kitchen chair under their feet. Eager to pass her magic tricks on to the next generation of holiday hosts, she shares her sneaky little tricks for making easy recipes look spectacular.

Tiffany, author of *The Ultimate Kids' Cookbook,* is the founder of Peanut Blossom, an online community for busy moms who want real-world, family-tested, kid-friendly food. She provides ongoing creative inspiration, helping parents celebrate the everyday moments that become cherished childhood memories. You can find her work on *Country Living, Parents, Woman's Day,* BuzzFeed and Melissa & Doug's Play Time Press.

INDEX